IT'S
NOT
TOO
LATE

IT'S NOT TOO LATE

TONY EVANS

HARVEST HOUSE PUBLISHERS
EUGENE, OREGON

Cover by Writely Designed, Buckley, Washington

Cover photo by Jake Gard / Unsplash

Back-cover photo by Don Fuller

Formerly titled *God's Unlikely Path to Success*

IT'S NOT TOO LATE
Copyright © 2012 by Tony Evans
Published by Harvest House Publishers
www.harvesthousepublishers.com

ISBN 978-0-7369-6849-2 (pbk.)
ISBN 978-0-7369-6850-8 (eBook)

Library of Congress Cataloging-in-Publication Data
    Names: Evans, Tony, 1949-
    Title: It's not too late / Tony Evans.
    Other titles: God's unlikely path to success
    Description: Eugene, Oregon : Harvest House Publishers, 2016. | Includes
        index. | Rev. ed. of: God's unlikely path to success. c2012.
    Identifiers: LCCN 2015040174 | ISBN 9780736968492 (pbk.)
    Subjects: LCSH: Success—Religious aspects—Christianity. | Christian
        life—Biblical teaching. | Success—Biblical teaching. | Bible—Biography

Printed in the United States of America

16 17 18 19 20 21 22 23 24 / VP-NI / 10 9 8 7 6 5 4 3

*This book is gratefully dedicated to
all those discouraged believers
who are looking for a second chance.*

Acknowledgments

I want to thank my good friends at Harvest House Publishers—Bob Hawkins Jr., LaRae Weikert, and Nick Harrison—for their belief in this vision and their diligent work in bringing this book to completion.

Contents

Introduction

One of my greatest joys in life is the privilege of being a pastor. It's a responsibility I do not take lightly. As a pastor, I frequently walk with people through their hurts, pains, and disappointments.

Sometimes, in the midst of their pain, people will ask me, "Is it too late for me? Is it too late for God to do something with me?" Those questions come out of a deep place where people think their many failures have caused them to have forfeited their God-given destiny. When asked that question, I always have one response: "No, it's *not* too late. It's *never* too late for God."

God frequently uses broken people to accomplish His purposes on earth. Time after time in Scripture, we read about broken people whom God raised up in marvelous ways. He used Moses, a murderer, to deliver the Hebrew slaves. He used Jacob, a liar and a trickster, to fulfill His promise to Abraham. He even included Rahab, a harlot, in the messianic family line. If God redeemed their lives, He can redeem your life too.

Brokeness should *never* keep you bound. Rather, it should release you into a life of freedom. A truly broken person understands the reality of John 15:5, where Jesus says, "Apart from Me you can do nothing." A broken person who has learned to depend on God is a force to be reckoned with.

Yet when you're staring at your past, strewn with failure, it's difficult to see your bright future, just as it's difficult to drive when you're constantly looking in your rearview mirror. When you drive, you need to glance at your rearview mirror, but if you continue to look there, you will end up hurting yourself and the others around you. That's why the windshield is so much larger than the rearview mirror—the windshield shows you where you're headed, not where you've been.

Halftime and Hope

If you've ever watched a football game, you know that midway through the game, the teams go to their respective locker rooms for halftime. Halftime is a time for rest and assessment. It's a time to regroup—to evaluate how things have been going and to decide what adjustments need to be made for the rest of the game.

The first half of any football game is important, but it is not determinative. Numerous teams over the years were ahead at halftime only to eventually lose the game. And numerous teams were losing at halftime, but by the time the game ended, they had turned things around. Until the final whistle is blown, the game is still up for grabs.

The same is true in life. You might be in your first or second quarter or heading into halftime, but if you are still here, the game of life is not over. Your clock is still ticking. There is plenty of life yet to live. Not only that, but your first half doesn't have to determine the outcome of the game. Maybe you've made mistakes and poor decisions; perhaps you've experienced many disappointments and failures. Maybe life has dealt you a harsh blow here or there. *But you are still here.* And as long as you're still here, the whistle has not blown and it is not too late for God to take you straight to the plan

He has for you. It is not too late for God to lead you into your glorious tomorrow!

See, God looks at your future while the enemy tries to keep you focused on your past. God says, "You *can* in spite of what has been done!" But the enemy says, "You *can't* because of what you've done!" God will never define you by your past, but the enemy will try to confine you by your past. Whether it's the good, the bad, or the ugly that dominates your first half, Satan's goal is to keep you chained there. But my charge to you as we go through these pages together is to never let your yesterday keep you from your tomorrow. Learn from yesterday—just don't live in it.

Once a Hillbilly, Always a Hillbilly?

Do you remember Jed Clampett and *The Beverly Hillbillies*? What made that TV show so interesting is that Jed and his family had been delivered from their past—a life of poverty and hillbillydom back in the Ozarks—but even after they moved to Beverly Hills, they continued to live their hillbilly ways. Their location had changed, but their mindset hadn't. The Clampetts' past devalued both a valuable present and a valuable future.

The same was true for the Israelites who escaped from 430 years of control by the Egyptians. The Israelites had left Egypt, but Egypt had not left them. As they sent spies into the Promised Land, they stood on the precipice of a glorious tomorrow, but because they chose to focus on the challenges they would face in that Promised Land, they grumbled and complained, wanting to go back to their past instead. "At least we had leeks, onions, fish, and plenty to eat in Egypt," they whined, choosing to look at life through their rearview mirror rather than focusing on the promises up ahead.

When God delivered the Israelites from Egypt, He delivered them *from* their past and *into* their future—Canaan. Yet because they chose to be so focused on yesterday, they missed their tomorrow. As a result, they had to wander in the wilderness for 40 years so God could disconnect them from their past. Many of us cannot get to our tomorrows because we are still carrying baggage from our past.

The Israelites remained tethered to their past because they failed to do what Hebrews 4:1-2 tells us is essential if we are to enter into the destiny God has for us—we must combine God's Word with faith.

> Therefore, let us fear if, while a promise remains of entering His rest, any one of you may seem to have come short of it. For indeed we have had good news preached to us, just as they also; but the word they heard did not profit them, because it was not united by faith in those who heard.

Faith means acting on God's Word. Faith is acting as if something *is* so even when it is *not* so in order for it to *be* so simply because God *said* so. Faith is always an action. That's why we're told to walk by faith and not to talk by faith. Until a truth from God's Word has been put into action in your life, it will be merely a spiritual theory. It will not be a concrete experience. Without an action, it will die in the wilderness. God is not as interested in your "amen" as He is in your action.

If you want a bag of cement to become concrete, you have to mix it with water. Likewise, you have to mix God's Word with faith in order for it to become a concrete experience in your life. The Word of God can make you feel good and give you an emotional high, but those feelings won't last long if the Word isn't mixed with faith. Faith demands an action, not just a feeling.

The people of Israel could have walked to Canaan in 35 days. But what should have taken 35 days ended up taking 40 years because they kept looking back. Maybe that sounds familiar to you. Maybe you expected to be further along in your life by now—further in your career, your relationships, your family, your finances, or even your emotional and spiritual well-being—but instead you keep looking back. You keep saying, "What if…why…but…" and everything else that can be said about yesterday.

You fear that you have blown it. You have missed your opportunity. You have failed. Or you fear that someone else has messed you up too much, that he has stolen your future or your hope. Yesterday is real to you. And it certainly *is* real. I'm not suggesting your past isn't real. But you need to stop looking at the leeks and the fish of your yesterday and instead look ahead to the milk and honey of your destiny. God gave the spies a glimpse of their tomorrow, and He has given you a glimpse of what He has in store for you too. It's a glimpse of a good future with a hope.

Unlike the Israelites in the wilderness, the individuals we're about to study in this book acted in faith in response to God's Word. As a result, many of them have been memoralized in the Hebrews 11 Hall of Faith, and all are remembered for having fulfilled God's calling on their lives. God is waiting for you to join them in taking the leap of faith into His arms of grace.

It's Not Too Late

Hospital maternity wards are some of the most optimistic places on earth. With four children and ten grandchildren (at the time of this writing—the number of grandchildren keeps growing!), I have had the opportunity to get to know the maternity ward pretty well.

As noses press against the window and eyes look down at the newborns, you can hear parents, grandparents, family, and friends express their congratulations, joy, expectations, and hopes for the babies. Hope springs eternal in the maternity ward—as it should. We want to believe that our sons, daughters, relatives, or friends will one day grow up to change the world, win the Super Bowl, write a bestselling novel, or become the president of the United States.

Though many hearts overflow with hope on that day of birth, not everyone will see their dreams come true as the days turn into years and the years turn into a lifetime. Life has a way of throwing us curveballs, handing us difficulties, and presenting us with challenges that can strip the wind right out of our sails.

When this happens, many of us long for a do-over. Just as children often shout, "Do-over!" when they don't like the way something turned out, we long for another chance. We long to stand before life and say, "Do-over!" But the reality is that we can't change the past. Because of this, many people are stuck in their present simply because they are stuck in their past. And even though Christians frequently claim the miracle-working, unlimited power of God, most think that even God isn't in the business of giving do-overs.

It is true—even God can't (or won't) change your past. But He can change your future, and that truth alone should give you hope. There is always hope when you have God on your side. Friend, if you hear anything from me over the course of this book, hear these four words: *It's not too late*.

As you read this book, I want you to experience this reality through the lives of people who could have thought it was too late for anything good to come of them. They may have done something, such as make a bad decision, or something may have been done to them. Regardless, it was not too late for God to turn their mess into a miracle.

It was not too late for Jonah. He ignored God's command to preach a call of repentance to the people of Ninevah and ended up in the belly of a whale. But God rescued a repentant Jonah, who went on to lead one of the greatest revivals of all time.

It was not too late for Samson. He turned his back on his vows to God and partied with the Philistine women. He lost his supernatural strength because of his sin, but in his brokenness, he called on God one last time, and God used him to defeat his enemies.

It was not too late for Sarah. Sarah doubted God's promise that she would give birth to a son, laughing at the news because of her old age. She plotted a human solution in a failed attempt to bring about a supernatural promise, but God in His mercy fulfilled the promise in Sarah's latter years.

It was not too late for Peter. Despite a defiant declaration that he would never leave Jesus, Peter denied Christ three times. But Peter's life was restored spiritually, and he went on to accomplish things the fisherman could never have imagined.

It was not too late for Rahab, Jacob, or Esther either, and it is definitely not too late for you. God has a purpose, a destiny, and a goal for your life. Don't go backward on Him now. You've come too far. You can't change your past regardless of how much you may want to. But your past does not have to determine your future. It's not too late to live in the hope and the high calling that are yours in Jesus Christ.

Regardless of what you have done, regardless of what others have done to you, and regardless of the depth of the pit you're in, God can still restore and use you. *It is not too late.* But don't take my word for it. Read on. Join me on this journey as we go deeper into the lives of broken people who left us a legacy of faith.

1

Moses Was a Murderer

Moses was a murderer. It doesn't get much worse than that. At the age of 40, Moses killed a man, and as a result he was snatched straight from the heart of Egyptian luxury and dropped in the middle of a desert called Midian to babysit sheep for the next 40 years.

What a detour!

Bad decisions can cause our lives to veer off course—not only for a year or two but for decades. Rebounding seems like an impossible feat, but that's exactly what Moses had to do.

If you've spent much time with sheep, you know that sheep don't make for very stimulating company. In fact, more than likely, Moses was frustrated and bored by the sheep. How else can you explain the fact that in Egypt, Moses was "a man of power in words and deeds" (Acts 7:22), but later he argued with God's call on his life—not once but twice—because he was "slow of speech and slow of tongue" (Exodus 4:10) and "unskilled in speech" (Exodus 6:12)? Those are two completely opposite realities. You can't be both "a man of power in words" and "unskilled in speech" at the same time.

Something happened to Moses in Midian. It wasn't simply that he got old, his bones began to ache more than they used to, or his hair turned gray. In Midian, Moses lost touch with who he was. He lost his confidence. He forgot his own potential. Or as I like to say, Moses lost his mojo.

You've probably never murdered anyone, but you may have lost your mojo somewhere along the way. If you don't know what I mean by *mojo*, it's simply that spark, energy, and enthusiasm that makes you, *you*.

Maybe you once made a decision that put your life on the wrong track, and you have regretted it to this day. Instead of blazing through life, the best you can hope for is a little flicker now and then.

I imagine that early on, like most people, you had dreams. You had a vision. You knew what you were good at and the skills you could use to make a difference in the world. In fact, you may even have thought you could take on the world. But then you found yourself in Midian, and as time went by and you kept dealing with the same sheep day in and day out, kept going to the same watering hole day in and day out, kept hearing the same complaints of rocky paths and itchy wool day in and day out, the spark inside you fizzled out.

If it has, I'm going to ask you to trust me—not because of who I am but because of who God is. The stories on these pages are not my stories. These are God's stories, and He preserved them for you and me to encourage us. So that's my question to you—will you do it? Will you trust me? Because what I'm about to tell you can change your life. God's truth has the power to do just that.

Moses Lost His Mojo

The first thing I want to tell you is that if you have lost your mojo, you are in excellent company. We mentioned that the same thing happened to Moses—one of the greatest heroes of the Bible. When the time was ripe for Moses to fulfill his life's calling and lead a few million people out of bondage and into freedom, he didn't even want to answer the call. "How are they going to believe me? Pharaoh won't listen to me," Moses argued. He sounded like a teenager throwing a fit because he doesn't want to do his chores. "You've got the wrong man, God. The people didn't listen to me, and Pharaoh won't either," Moses said in my Tony Evans paraphrase of Exodus 6:12.

But Moses was wrong. And you're wrong too if you believe God can't or won't use you. Friend, God has a plan for you and a plan for me, just as He had a plan for Moses. His plan for you may not include leading a few million people out of slavery, but His plan is good because He's a good God. It's a plan with a future and a hope.

If Moses can rebound after 40 years on the sideline, you can too. In fact, it's because of Moses and his rebound that I'm writing this book for you. With so much to learn from his life and the lives of the others we're going to look at, no one should *ever* think that it's too late for God to turn things around. If you have thought about giving up, throwing in the towel, or dismissing yourself from making any meaningful contribution in life, *don't*. It's not too late. Remember what I asked you to do? Trust me. Not because of me but because of God and the truths I'm about to share with you.

Now, I'm not going to argue with you—maybe you did make a wrong choice or many wrong choices. And maybe your situation does look bleak from the outside, from the inside, or both. But I doubt it looks any worse than an old man in Midian walking with sheep every day.

You're still here, still reading this page, so it's not too late for God to do something amazing in and through you. God is the great unfigure-outable God, and His ways are much higher than our ways. Never look at your circumstances. Never look at yourself. Chances are your view of yourself and your circumstances has become distorted, just as Moses' was.

Instead, I want you to focus on God. See what He does with each of the lives we are going to look at in this book. And when you do, I want you to dare to hope again. Dare to dream again. Dare to pick up your mojo and put it on again. God turned Moses' hopeless desert situation completely around, and He can turn your situation around too.

The Making of Moses

Scripture tells us that from the time Moses entered the world, a Hebrew baby born to a slave family at the height of Egypt's domination and rule, he was a beautiful child. Something special about Moses made people willing to risk punishment from the Egyptian leaders in order to save him.

Exodus 1 explains that at that time, a new Pharaoh had risen to power in Egypt. He "did not know Joseph," the Israelite who had played a critical role at a time of extended national famine (Exodus 1:8). Joseph's plan had saved the Egyptians and many of the people in the surrounding nations, including his own father and brothers and their families.

Before long, the 70 Hebrews (not counting wives) who had come to live in Egypt had multiplied so much that Pharaoh felt threatened. So Pharaoh made a decision. "The people of the sons of Israel are more and mightier than we. Come, let us deal wisely with them, or else they will multiply and in the event of war, they will also join themselves to those who hate us, and fight against us and depart from the land" (verses 9-10).

At first, the plan was to wear out the Hebrew people through hard labor, hoping not only to discourage them but also to reduce their number. Pharaoh must have assumed that if the Hebrews were exhausted from working, they wouldn't have the incentive, strength, or time to continue populating the land. The Egyptians "appointed taskmasters over them to afflict them with hard labor. And they built for Pharaoh storage cities, Pithom and Raamses" (verse 11).

But the more the Egyptians tried to wear out the Hebrews, "the more they multiplied and the more they spread out" (verse 12). As a result, the Egyptians increased their oppression, making the Hebrews' lives "bitter with hard labor in mortar and bricks and at all kinds of labor in the field" (verse 14).

Still not having reduced the number of Hebrew births in his land as much as he had hoped to, Pharaoh decided to reduce that number himself. He "spoke to the Hebrew midwives, one of whom was named Shiphrah and the other was named Puah; and he said, 'When you are helping the Hebrew women to give birth and see them upon the birthstool, if it is a son, then you shall put him to death'" (verses 15-16). But the Bible tells us, "The midwives feared God, and did not do as the king of Egypt had commanded them, but let the boys live" (verse 17).

So Pharaoh broadened his attack and declared, "Every son who is born you are to cast into the Nile" (verse 22). This is what eventually happened to baby Moses, although he wasn't exactly "cast" into the Nile. Instead, Moses' mother found "a wicker basket and covered it over with tar and pitch. Then she put the child into it and set it among the reeds by the bank of the Nile" (Exodus 2:3).

It just so happened that while Moses was floating in the river in his wicker basket, Pharaoh's daughter came by. While bathing in the Nile, she saw the basket and asked her maid to go get it and bring it to her.

> When she opened it, she saw the child, and behold, the boy was crying. And she had pity on him and said, "This is one of the Hebrews' children." Then his sister said to Pharaoh's daughter, "Shall I go and call a nurse for you from the Hebrew women that she may nurse the child for you?" Pharaoh's daughter said to her, "Go ahead." So the girl went and called the child's mother. Then Pharaoh's daughter said to her, "Take this child away and

nurse him for me and I will give you your wages." So the woman took the child and nursed him (Exodus 2:6-9).

Talk about a turnaround! One minute baby Moses is about to be killed, and the next minute he is growing up in Pharaoh's house and his own mother is paid to raise him! In the book of Acts, we get a glimpse into the boy that the writer of Acts calls "no ordinary child" (Acts 7:20 NIV). We read, "Moses was educated in all the wisdom of the Egyptians and was powerful in speech and action (verse 22 NIV). In other words, Moses was living large. He went to the best schools and had the best education and the best opportunities.

Moses never had to worry about finances or whether he would be wearing name-brand clothes. He had culture, skills, and power. In fact, as a trusted member of Pharaoh's household, he was in line to become a powerful ruler in Egypt.

But something happened when Moses turned 40 that would forever change his life.

> Now it came about in those days, when Moses had grown up, that he went out to his brethren and looked on their hard labors; and he saw an Egyptian beating a Hebrew, one of his brethren. So he looked this way and that, and when he saw there was no one around, he struck down the Egyptian and hid him in the sand (Exodus 2:11-12).

Moses remembered what he had been told about who he was. We don't know who told him, but there is a good chance that Moses' mother whispered in his ear, "You're not one of them," as she took care of him. "You are one of us, Moses," she might have said. "You're an Israelite." We know Moses knew because we read that Moses went out to his "brethren." In fact, the passage mentions the word *brethren* twice, making certain that we don't miss that Moses knew he was an Israelite and not an Egyptian.

Curious about his people and seeking to identify with them, Moses decided to be associated with the people of God rather than live large in Egypt. He was committed. He was determined. He was even powerful. He just didn't know the right way to do what he wanted to do.

> When Moses was forty years old, he decided to visit his own people, the Israelites. He saw one of them being mistreated by an Egyptian, so he went to his defense and avenged him by killing the Egyptian. Moses thought that his own people would realize that God was using him to rescue them, but they did not (Acts 7:23-25 NIV).

Moses thought wrong, so he acted wrong. Moses saw an Egyptian messing with one of his brothers and said, "I'm not going to let you get away with this. I'm going to be the one who delivers my people, and I'm going to start right now with you!" Moses did what a lot of us do—he used human means to accomplish a divine goal. He used his own orientation and perspective to go after a legitimate outcome. Moses didn't try to stop the fight. He avenged the Israelite by killing the Egyptian.

Now, I'm not quite sure what Moses' long-term plan was. I don't know if he thought he was going to deliver the Israelites one Egyptian at a time or if he was just making a point. As a highly visible member of Pharaoh's household, Moses knew that he could get attention just by standing there. That's why the Scripture points out that he "looked this way and that, and when he saw there was no one around, he struck down the Egyptian and hid him in the sand" (Exodus 2:12). Feeling secure that no one had seen him, Moses must have thought he had begun the process of showing where his commitment was. He was truly the Israelites' hero, sent to deliver them from their oppression. Yet the next day, when Moses tried to stop a fight between two Israelites, they refused his help. He wasn't trying to kill them too. Moses was just saying, "Brothers, can't we all get along?"

Instead, they said, "Who made you ruler and judge over us? Are you thinking of killing me as you killed the Egyptian yesterday?" (Acts 7:27 NIV). One of two things must have happened the day before. Moses might not have noticed that somebody was watching. But more likely, the guy he rescued and avenged started talking.

So now Moses has two problems. First, he has just committed first-degree murder. And it *was* murder because as a respected leader, he didn't have to kill the Egyptian to stop the fight. Second, the folks he had come to help have rejected him. So Moses has two things from which to rebound. But before he even gets a chance to try, word about what he had done spreads to the Egyptians, even to Pharaoh himself. We read, "When Pharaoh heard of this matter, he tried to kill Moses. But Moses fled from the presence of Pharaoh and settled in the land of Midian, and he sat down by a well" (Exodus 2:15).

So now we find Moses, a solitary fugitive, sitting by a well in the middle of a desert.

Before we go any further I want to make sure you don't check out by telling me, "But Tony, I've never killed anyone!" According to Jesus, physical murder is not the only kind of murder. That's just the obvious kind. Jesus goes so far as to say that a person should not even project anger toward another. Maybe that anger doesn't physically take a life, but it begins a process of taking things from that life.

Anger can show up in a variety of ways. It shows up when a person's character is destroyed or lessened by another person who is angry at him or her. It shows up when someone isn't able to advance at work or in a community or at church because someone else is holding them back. It can show up in the home when one spouse seeks to control or dominate the other spouse out of anger. Or a parent damages a child's esteem through angry outbursts or unrealistic expectations. Anger can show up everywhere—not just in Egypt. It does its damage in the workforce, at home, in the church, and in the community in a number of ways, attempting to take away people's opportunities and kill their potential.

So my question to you is, has your anger ever hurt or damaged someone? If so, then from a spiritual standpoint, Moses' story applies to you too. It's really not that difficult to be considered a murderer in the kingdom of God. You might not be sitting by a well in Midian, but spiritual consequences show up in other ways.

Moses' world changed in two days, and our worlds can change just as fast.

This reminds me of an implosion I saw on the news recently. A couple of very old buildings in Dallas had been quarantined to be imploded so that builders could make room for a new building in that area. In less than 15 seconds, what had stood for years and years simply imploded and collapsed. Buildings that had taken large crews more than a year or two to build fell into a heap of rubble in less time than it probably will take for you to read this page. Life can happen that way sometimes too. Your life can be moving along without a care, and then in less than two sunsets, your whole world has fallen apart. It has collapsed, your dreams have died, and you are nowhere near where you thought you would be or where you wanted to be.

Moses went from the White House to the outhouse in just two days due to one missed shot, one miscalculation. As Moses tended those sheep in the wilderness day in and day out, I bet he looked back over his life, thinking that if he could just roll back the hands of time, he would have done things differently. He wouldn't have made *that* decision on *that* day with *that* person. He wouldn't have gone there, done that, said that, or failed to do or say one thing or another. If he could simply turn back time, he could turn things around himself. He could still live in Pharaoh's house, eat Pharaoh's food, go to Pharaoh's parties, use his Egyptian Visa card, and drive his Mercedes chariot. But now, in the desert, with Pharaoh intent on killing him, Moses no longer sees any hope for himself. He probably thinks—just as you might today—"It's too late for me. God can't use me after what I've done with my life."

In fact, when we come to the third chapter of Exodus, Moses is 80 years old. We have read in the book of Acts that when Moses killed the Egyptian, he was 40 years old. Yet when he has his next encounter with God, he is 80 years old (Acts 7:30). That's a 40-year time-out for one bad action. But when you think about it, that isn't all too unusual. I've been a pastor for 35 years, and as a result, I have spent a considerable amount of time counseling individuals and families through trials in their lives. It's not unusual to find out that bad decisions have triggered emotional, physical, attitudinal, or relational repercussions that have played out for decades. Just as Moses' life was changed dramatically, many other people's lives have changed, and the thought keeps creeping back, "If only I hadn't..."

Friend, if you're thinking of an "If only I hadn't..." situation right now, then I want you to pay extra close attention as we continue. Because of your past, you may think it's too late for you to dream, to hope, or to live with your mojo again. But it's never too late as long as God is still in the equation. And as long as you're still here, God is still in the equation because He hasn't gone anywhere.

At 80 years old, it would have been easy for Moses to think it was too late. At 80 years old, it was probably easy for Moses to think that nothing was ever going to change. At 80 years old, no doubt Moses thought that all of his tomorrows would be like his todays and that he was forever doomed to a miserable life of shepherding his father-in-law's sheep.

But at 80 years old, everything *did* change for Moses.

We read, "Now Moses was pasturing the flock of Jethro his father-in-law, the priest of Midian; and he led the flock to the west side of the wilderness and came to Horeb, the mountain of God" (Exodus 3:1).

Horeb, the mountain of God, is also known as Mount Sinai. Moses is about to have the encounter of his life, and the location of this encounter is critical. Mount Sinai is where God will later give Moses the Ten Commandments. It's known as the mountain of God because it's the place of God's presence. In other words, here Moses has an encounter that will set him free from his past and give him a brand-new future in the presence of God. Only when Moses took his flock to the mountain of God could he regain what he had lost.

If you are in a Moses-like situation and you've been living month after month or year after year with repercussions from your missed shots or wrong decisions, the first step to getting back on track is to find out what you really need.

You don't need another sermon. You don't need another Bible seminar or conference. To be honest, you don't even need another book. That doesn't mean I want you to put this one down just yet or stop going to church. Those things are good and important. But when you are in a Moses-like situation, you need a fresh encounter with God.

You need to be in God's presence. In God's presence, you're going to hear His word specifically for you rather than His general word for everyone. God explains in Joel 2:25-26 (NIV) what can happen in His presence.

> I will repay you for the years the locusts have eaten, the great locust and the young locust, the other locusts and the locust swarm—my great army that I sent among you. You will have plenty to eat, until you are full, and you will praise the name of the LORD your God, who has worked wonders for you.

The "locusts" had taken away 40 years of Moses' life because of the decision that he had made, yet God uses those 40 years to do what Moses could have never done without them. Before the wilderness, Moses thought he could deliver the Israelites one man at a time all by himself. After the wilderness, Moses had learned to depend on God. The consequences of Moses' mistake won't be removed, and the 40 years that were lost are forever lost, but the beauty of God is that He pours the *value* of those lost years into Moses' next 40 years.

But that transfer of value happened only when Moses went to

where God was, when he encountered His presence. The same is true for you and me. God promises to restore us when we return to Him, but that means more than listening to a sermon, going to a seminar, or singing a song—it means being desperate for Him in His presence.

When God Does Something Amazing

In God's presence, Moses got a special-effects light show. We read in Exodus 3:2, "The angel of the LORD appeared to him in a blazing fire from the midst of a bush; and he looked, and behold, the bush was burning with fire, yet the bush was not consumed." Moses experienced God's presence. In fact, "the angel of the LORD" is the preincarnate Christ, so Moses experienced God up close and personal.

You can learn a secret from this passage, a secret about how you can know when God is about to do something amazing in your life. This passage explains how you can know when God is getting ready to invade your ordinary with His extraordinary. Theologians have a fancy name for when God shows up that's taken from the early Jewish rabbis—*Shekinah*. *Shekinah*, transliterated from the Hebrew, literally means "to settle" or "to dwell." The Shekinah glory is the visible manifestation of God's presence. It's the way God makes Himself so visible to you that you *know* He is there.

Never in history have we seen God show up just to show up. When God shows up in a visible, Shekinah way, He is about to do something that will blow your mind. He invades your normal with His abnormal, creating a scenario that you can't explain. But keep in mind that when God does something that doesn't make sense, it's not supposed to make sense. There's no point in even trying to makes sense of it—just watch and see God in it.

Time after time in the Bible and in subsequent history, when God was getting ready to move in a seemingly hopeless situation, He showed up in a way that human understanding could not explain. It's important that you remember this. If you're in God's presence and you're looking for a change, then look for something that you cannot explain. God tells us in Isaiah 55:8-9 (NIV), "'For my thoughts are not your thoughts, neither are your ways my ways,' declares the LORD. 'As the heavens are higher than the earth, so are my ways higher than your ways and my thoughts than your thoughts.'"

That's how different God is from you and me. He is not like us. His ways are so high that we can't even see them. One of my all-time favorite vocal groups is the Delfonics, and if God had written this in the era of soul music, He would have framed that verse this way, "Didn't I blow your mind this time, didn't I? Didn't I show up in a way that you could not explain, didn't I?"

In the situation with Moses, God showed up in a bush that was on fire but did not burn up. It would be nothing special to see a bush on fire in a hot wilderness. Stuff gets dry in the wilderness, and fires start. But when a bush is on fire and does not burn up, that's different. That's the not-normal situation that God showed up in. And when He did, Moses said, "I must turn aside now and see this marvelous sight, why the bush is not burned up" (Exodus 3:3). Moses couldn't explain it, but he also couldn't ignore it. He called it a "marvelous sight," and you can bet he wanted to know what was going on with this weird bush.

And God told him. After Moses turned to look at the bush, God spoke. We read, "When the LORD saw that he turned aside to look, God called to him from the midst of the bush and said, 'Moses, Moses!'" (verse 4). God didn't reveal Himself to Moses until Moses turned aside to look. A lot of us want more from God, but we haven't turned to look at what He's already doing. We want God to show up, but we haven't responded to the way He has already shown up. And then we sit and complain and wonder why we don't get more.

One of the reasons we don't get more is that God hasn't seen us doing anything with what He has already given us. When God gives you something you have never seen before and cannot explain, don't ignore it. Turn and look for God in the midst of it because God just might be trying to reveal Himself to you at a whole new level.

This is what God did with Moses. When Moses turned aside, he heard two words: "Moses, Moses." Did God speak to him in Hebrew? Moses had been living in the desert of Midian as a foreigner for 40 years—had it been that long since he heard his name spoken in Hebrew? He'd been trapped in a wilderness for four decades with his life seemingly going nowhere, and out of a bush Moses heard God calling his name. This wasn't a general sermon or a general word for everybody. This was God talking directly to Moses because Moses' situation was so desperate that it demanded a personal word from God.

I've been preaching for nearly four decades myself, and I can no longer count the number of times someone has come up to me after a sermon that I delivered with no particular person in mind, and that individual will tell me that the sermon I just preached was meant exactly for them. In fact, just last week a lady came up to me after the sermon—someone I had never met—and she said, "Pastor, what you preached this morning was meant just for me. I was wrestling with a decision, and your sermon told me exactly what I needed to do." Now, I didn't know this lady's situation. I just preached what God had put on my heart for this particular Sunday. But when you are in God's presence, the Holy Spirit takes *the Word of God* and turns it into *a word from God* for you.

When you are sitting in a congregation, listening to a sermon on the radio or on your MP3 player, or reading a book and you feel as if you are the only one in the room or the only one this message was intended for, that's when God is calling your name…"Sarah, Sarah!" or "Keith, Keith!"

When you hear your name, do what Moses did. Moses said, "Here I am." I wish I could have been there because I doubt Moses uttered those words clearly. It was probably more of a manly grunt. He was looking at a bush that was burning and yet not burned up. He had just heard God speak directly to him—by name. It's a wonder that Moses was able to contain himself at all. In my Tony Evans paraphrase, he might have answered, "Me? Yeah! I'm here. Right here."

The reason I think that has to do with what comes next. God quickly replied, "Do not come near here" (verse 5). Moses had heard his name called after a 40-year silence, and he was ready to check this thing out. But instead God stops him right in his tracks and says, "Remove your sandals from your feet, for the place on which you are standing is holy ground" (verse 5).

God stops Moses and tells him to take off his shoes. To take off your shoes is to identify with who you are as a human. Man was originally made from the ground. God made Adam from the dust of the ground before He breathed life into him. So essentially, all mankind has originally come from the ground. When you or I die, much of our physical body will decay and return back into the ground. Taking off his shoes reminded Moses of who he was and how high he should stand in God's presence. Any shoe that Moses wore would have a sole on it. Even if that sole was just a quarter of an inch thick, that was still a quarter of an inch too high in God's presence.

Not only that, but on his best day, Moses needed to be reminded that he isn't much more than dignified dirt. Now, God can do a lot with dignified dirt, but God didn't want Moses to "think more highly of himself than he ought to think" (Romans 12:3).

"Moses, Moses!" God called out. "I want to remind you of who you are. Take off your shoes and connect with what you are really tied to—*dirt*." But the difference now is that this dirt is special dirt because this dirt is holy dirt. Holy dirt on holy ground is something that God can do something marvelous with.

After 40 years of leading dumb sheep through a barren wilderness, Moses probably thought it was too late to do anything significant—especially something like his long-lost dream of helping the Israelites to freedom. But Moses didn't know that God had been preparing him all along. First God gave him 40 years of "uptown" preparation in the luxury of Egypt. Next God gave him 40 years of "downtown" preparation in the isolation of Midian. The second 40 years of preparation came about because of Moses' wrong choice, but that didn't stop God from using it. Moses would need the skills he learned leading sheep in the wilderness to lead the sheep of Israel out of Egypt and toward the Promised Land.

The consequences that Moses suffered were no doubt painful, and the days, nights, weeks, months, and years were certainly long, but God has a unique way of turning a mess into a miracle. We learn from the life of Moses that God doesn't always relieve the consequences or erase the pain, but He is so big that He won't even let your mess mess Him up. He still has a plan and a calling for you. If you will seek Him, you will find it just as Moses did when God showed up in his wilderness.

But the interesting thing about the timing of Moses' calling is that it didn't happen until something else happened in Egypt. Keep in mind that God is never just working with you. God is always doing more than one thing at a time. God was preparing Moses in the wilderness during his 40-year hiatus, but He was also waiting on an entire nation to cry out to Him for deliverance. Essentially, Israel needed to *want* to be delivered. They were enjoying Egypt too much. But when they cried out, God spoke to Moses.

The Bible has been divided by verses and chapters in order to help us keep our place as we read it. But when the Bible was written, it didn't have verses or chapters. Chapter 2 in Exodus closes with this:

> Now it came about in the course of those many days that the king of Egypt died. And the sons of Israel sighed because of the bondage, and they cried out; and their cry for help because of their bondage rose up to God. So God heard their groaning; and God remembered

His covenant with Abraham, Isaac, and Jacob. God saw the sons of Israel, and God took notice of them (Exodus 2:23-25).

Exodus 3 begins, "Now Moses was pasturing the flock of Jethro his father-in-law, the priest of Midian; and he led the flock to the west side of the wilderness and came to Horeb, the mountain of God."

In the original language of the Bible, there is no chapter division. When the Israelites cried out to God and God took notice of them, God showed up to Moses in a burning bush on His mountain. While God was working with Israel, He was also working with Moses to bring a broken man back to a broken nation in order to accomplish a marvelous exodus to freedom. God is always hooking stuff up.

After his 40-year detour from a missed shot, Moses went into God's presence. He responded to God's person. He got God's program. And soon he will experience God's power because when God shows up in Egypt, He will display power that Moses never knew in the desert. But even what Moses learned will be used in his calling to lead God's people to freedom because God never wastes a thing.

Just as it wasn't too late for God to call Moses, it's not too late for God to redeem your situation and use you in a way you may not fathom right now. Don't ever become satisfied with where you are in the wilderness, even if it was your mistake or sin that got you there.

God holds the all-time record for most successful rebounds, but you need to position yourself in His presence in order to see the marvelous thing He's going to do. You need to turn and look in His direction in order for Him to call you by name and recommission you to service.

And when He does, you will have what we used to call in the old church down home a testimony. You will have a testimony, like Moses, of what God can do when it looks like there's nothing else that can possibly be done to redeem your situation.

2

Rahab Was a Harlot

Rahab was a harlot. She wasn't a secret-agent harlot, either. In fact, anyone who knew Rahab also knew what she was about. Even the Bible doesn't mince words when it tells us about "a harlot whose name was Rahab" (Joshua 2:1).

Rahab sold her body for money. I can't put it any more clearly. She let men have full reign over her body in exchange for some cold hard cash.

After enough time earning money that way, most anyone would stop dreaming about her future. With a reputation like that, most anyone would give up hopes of finding the right man to marry. With a day-in and day-out, night-in and night-out job like that, most anyone would assume that the one true God, whose presence is unapproachably holy, would have no intention of ever approaching her.

Rahab was a harlot—a member of the oldest profession in the world, a profession known by different names depending on who's talking about it. Some people would call Rahab a prostitute. Others would call her a whore. Some would call her Rahab the hussy or maybe an escort. A lady of the evening, a hooker, or even a ho. Whatever the name, they all mean the same thing: Rahab made a career out of servicing men with sexual favors.

One day a woman was asked by a man if she would sell herself for one night for a million dollars. She said she would have to think about it. He then changed the question. "Would you sell yourself for five dollars?" he asked.

"Five dollars?" she replied, "What do you think I am?"

"We've already determined what you are," he answered. "Right now we're just trying to determine the price."

See, a lot of us define what Rahab did as different from what many of us do—men or women. If a man takes a lady out to dinner and then "charges" her for the meal, and she offers payment through sexual gratification, it's the same thing but simply with different terms of agreement. If a woman gives herself to a man she is not married to in order to feel secure or gain his attention because she doesn't want to be alone, it's the same thing but simply with different methods of payment. If a man tries to conquer a woman or several women through illicit sex so that he will feel more powerful or in control, it is the same thing.

Sex outside of marriage is a barter regardless of how you look at it. Without the committed covenant of marriage, an exchange is being made. It's a trade. In fact, at times, sex might also be a trade inside a marriage that isn't operating according to mutual respect and covenantal love.

When we strip away the veneer from what many people have done or are doing and we see it for what it is, we realize that it isn't that different from Rahab's occupation. The conditions, frequency, and labels may be different, but that's all.

But as we saw with Moses, and as we will see with Rahab the harlot, it's never too late and the pit is never too deep for God to restore us, redeem us, and turn our dire situations 180 degrees.

Two Spies and a Call Girl

Rahab's name begins with the word *Ra*, which was the name of a false Egyptian god representing the sun or creative powers. A Canaanite, Rahab was obviously raised in a pagan environment surrounded by the cultural strongholds of her day. These and other influences led her to adopt a lifestyle of indignity.

We're told that she had set up her place of business in an easily accessible location. "Her house was on the city wall, so that she was living on the wall" (Joshua 2:15). Rahab had followed the first three rules of real estate: location, location, and location. Travelers passing through or citizens heading out could easily find Rahab's place. This might also be one of the reasons the two spies who had been sent by Joshua to examine the land chose Rahab's house. Suspicions as to why the two Israelites were in the city would definitely be lower if seen in a place like Rahab's.

The spies, wanting to be as inconspicuous as possible, found a location where strangers would frequently go—a local brothel. However, somebody saw them go into Rahab's house and reported it to the king. The king sent emissaries to smoke them out. Everyone knows that if the king gives the order to turn someone over to him and you refuse, the penalty is death. This wasn't a suggestion. Rahab now faced a grave decision—would she turn the spies over to her king, or would she hide them, risking her own life?

Rahab chose not to reveal the presence of the men. Even though her life was at stake, she hid the men on her roof while telling the emissaries they had just missed them. "If you hurry, you might catch them," Rahab said, pointing in the general direction that she was pretending they had gone. Rahab chose to risk her life in order to protect their lives. As we will see later, Rahab did this because she had heard about the God that these men served, and she feared Him.

After the king's men left Rahab's house, she went up to the rooftop, where she had hidden the two spies from Israel. We read what she said in Joshua 2:9-11.

> I know that the LORD has given you the land, and that the terror of you has fallen on us, and that all the inhabitants of the land have melted away before you. For we have heard how the LORD dried up the water of the Red Sea before you when you came out of Egypt, and what you did to the two kings of the Amorites who were beyond the Jordan, to Sihon and Og, whom you utterly destroyed. When we heard it, our hearts melted and no courage remained in any man any longer because of you; for the LORD your God, He is God in heaven above and on earth beneath.

In essence, Rahab let them know, "We know all about you guys. In fact, we've known about you for 40 years. Since God opened up the Red Sea 40 years ago, we have been afraid of you. We're scared of your God and His reputation. So that's why I hid you—because your God is the God of heaven and earth."

Rahab's faith controlled her function. She made a choice to hide the two Israelite men rather than to satisfy the king. She chose to identify with the people who belonged to God because she feared God more than man.

We read in Hebrews 11:31 that Rahab's decision to take in the spies was an act of faith: "*By faith* Rahab the harlot did not perish along with those who were disobedient, after she had welcomed the spies in peace." Clearly, Rahab's decision was made because of faith in what she believed to be true. It's important to recognize that faith is more than a feeling. Faith is a function. Just as Rahab's risky move to hide the spies revealed her faith, you need to look at your actions in order to know that you have faith. Don't look at your feelings because your feelings will fluctuate. A person can be a man of faith or a woman of faith without ever having feelings of faith. Faith has to do with your feet. Feet, not feelings, prove whether or not you actually have faith.

Rahab may have had very strong feelings. Scripture doesn't tell us, but she could have been scared to death when the emissaries showed up. Rahab knew the consequences of hiding foreigners when a king has requested them to be turned over. I imagine Rahab's heart was pounding when she went to open the door. Her mouth may have gotten suddenly dry and her eyes widened.

Trying her best to appear calm and normal, she might have forced her words out of a parched throat, hoping all along that the king's officials wouldn't notice her hands were shaking as she pointed in the direction she wanted to send them.

The Bible doesn't say, so until we get to heaven we will never know what Rahab was feeling that day. But we do know what she did. Rahab took action. She acted in faith. Rahab made a decision to let her feet reflect what she believed to be true. Rahab's actions were intentional. And because they were, she made a request. We read about her plea in Joshua 2:12-13.

> Now therefore, please swear to me by the LORD, since I have dealt kindly with you, that you also will deal kindly with my father's household, and give me a pledge of truth, and spare my father and my mother and my brothers and my sisters, with all who belong to them, and deliver our lives from death.

In other words, Rahab said, "I know we're about to get massacred, so I want to cut a deal with your God right now. When you come and tear this place apart, I want to know that you have my back because I had yours." Rahab cut a deal with God's people. She asked for kindness.

Two things stand out. First, Rahab said the word *also*. She reminded the spies that she had just spared their lives, dealing kindly with them. In response, she asked them to deal kindly with her and her family. She emphasized that this was a two-way, reciprocal arrangement. Rahab's profession had taught her how to work two-way arrangements.

The second thing to point out is the word Rahab chose to use, which the English Bibles have translated as "kindly." The Hebrew word, however, doesn't merely mean "being nice" or "friendly." Rahab wasn't asking the Israelites to be polite as they ambushed her town. Instead, Rahab chose the Hebrew word *chesed*. *Chesed* means "kindness," but it also means "loyalty" and "faithfulness." This word is used more than 200 times in the Old Testament, referring specifically to how an agreement should be approached attitudinally. More than any other word in the Bible, *chesed* is used to reflect the terms of a covenant between two parties. Most often, it defines God's covenantal covering in spite of Israel's unfaithfulness. When a person has God's *chesed*, that person has the backing of a covenant.

Rahab said she wanted a covenant—a loyal love. She wanted kindness that extended beyond emotion or even duty; one that offered a covering of loyalty. She wanted an agreement that she could count on. And she wanted it because of the action she had done by faith.

A Lesson on Faith from a Harlot

It's interesting that one of the greatest lessons in the Bible on faith is given to us by a harlot. In fact, I'm not the one who keeps bringing up the fact that Rahab was a harlot. I'm simply following the Scripture. Rahab is called a harlot nearly each and every time she's mentioned in the Bible. Even James notes her occupation about 1500 years later in the New Testament when he talks about her as an example of true faith. This sister can't seem to get a break.

Yet even with the title of harlot, what James says about her is important for all of us seeking to be used by God, because it demonstrates the powerful connection between faith and function.

What use is it, my brethren, if someone says he has faith but he has no works? Can that faith save him? If a brother or sister is without clothing and in need of daily food, and one of you says to them, "Go in peace, be warmed and be filled," and yet you do not give them what is necessary for their body, what use is that? Even so faith, if it has no works, is dead being by itself (James 2:14-17).

Keep in mind that James isn't talking about the faith that's needed to go to heaven. James is talking to believers who are on their way to heaven. He refers to them directly in this passage as "my brethren." Not only that, but James opens his letter by addressing it to "the twelve tribes who are dispersed abroad," indicating that his intended audience is Jewish. Further, in chapters 2 and 5, James speaks to them directly as followers of Christ:

My brethren, do not hold your faith in our glorious Lord Jesus Christ with an attitude of personal favoritism (James 2:1).

Therefore be patient, brethren, until the coming of the Lord. The farmer waits for the precious produce of the soil, being patient about it, until it gets the early and late rains. You too be patient; strengthen your hearts, for the coming of the Lord is near (James 5:7-8).

When James writes about faith in the passage we looked at in chapter 2, he is talking about another kind of salvation. His listeners are already saved for eternity. James is writing about God's saving power *on earth*. According to Strong's concordance, the Greek word James uses is *sozo*, literally meaning to "make well, heal, restore." James is specifically referring to God's restoring power in history, not His saving power for eternity.

Salvation for eternity comes by faith alone in Christ alone. That kind of faith will get a person to heaven. But a lot of us know people who are going to heaven but who are no earthly good down here. Maybe you know people who will make it to glory but who have never seen what happens when glory comes to earth. These people never have a testimony of how God broke into a situation and turned it around supernaturally by His saving power. So they look forward to heaven simply because they can't stand life on earth.

Maybe you not only *know* people like that but actually *are* like that. You know that God has promised you an abundant life, but every day seems empty and meaningless—as if you're just going through the motions. You hear how God showed up in the life of your friend or of someone at your church, and you read about Him in the Bible, but you've never experienced Him for yourself. Or if you did, it was so long ago you can't remember it anymore.

James tells us that one reason we don't see God invade our ordinary with His extraordinary is that we don't live our lives with faith. We don't take the step of faith, like Rahab did, to show with our choices that we're putting our trust in God alone. We don't live our lives with actions that back up what we say we believe. When we do live a life of faith, James tells us what happens.

> And the scripture was fulfilled that says, "Abraham believed God, and it was credited to him as righteousness," and he was called God's friend. You see that a person is considered righteous by what they do and not by faith alone.
>
> In the same way, was not even Rahab the prostitute considered righteous for what she did when she gave lodging to the spies and sent them off in a different direction? As the body without the spirit is dead, so faith without deeds is dead (James 2:23-25 NIV).

First, James tells us that Abraham's faith was credited to him as righteousness and made him God's friend. Becoming God's friend is the best thing that could happen to you. When Rahab put her trust in God through her actions, she received the *chesed* (covenant love) that a loyal friend would give. God is a God of love, and God loves everyone, but nowhere do we see that God is everyone's *friend*. In fact, Jesus makes a clear distinction when talking to His disciples.

> You are my friends *when* you do the things I command you. I'm no longer calling you servants because servants don't understand what their master is thinking and planning. No, I've named you friends because I've let you in on everything I've heard from the Father (John 15:14-15 MSG).

Jesus said that when you do what He asks, He is not only your Master, Lord, and Savior but also your friend. And as a friend, He does what friends do—He whispers His secrets to you. He tells you what God tells Him. I can't imagine any greater friendship than one with the God of the universe, who knows the end from the beginning, the outside from the inside, the up from the down…and who is willing to let you in on all of it. That is a saving friendship, a restoring friendship. That kind of friendship can bring healing, peace, protection, and purpose. But that kind of friendship comes through faith—actions that demonstrate obedience to Christ's commands. If God had written Gary Chapman's bestselling book *The Five Love Languages*, He might have added a sixth. God's love language is faith.

James tells us that when Rahab took the spies into her home and hid them on her roof so she could send them out safely after the king's emissaries had left, this work done in faith saved her. It delivered her from an undeliverable situation. Not only that, but Rahab's faith delivered her family too.

James tells us that Rahab's faith did this by making a hooker holy. Her faith made a prostitute righteous. It put her in the same chapter as the patriarch Abraham—in Scripture's Hall of Faith in

Hebrews 11. She was God's friend, covered with *chesed*—loyal love manifested on earth. Rahab's faith delivered her not only for eternity but also in history.

One of the reasons many of us aren't seeing God come through for us in our day-to-day lives is that God hasn't seen our faith. He hasn't seen our actions demonstrate that we truly believe what we say or feel about Him. The only validation for faith in your life is that your actions back up what you believe.

I want to be careful to repeat that I'm not talking about the faith it takes to get a believer to heaven. I'm talking about the faith it takes to get heaven to join you on earth, on your job, in your relationships, in your career, in your health, and anywhere you need to witness God's supernatural power. That kind of friendship with God requires a faith that shows up in your feet.

Too many Christians are going to have culture shock when they get to heaven because they never experienced God's power and presence on earth. But not Rahab. Rahab saw God's eternal power enter her temporal situation, delivering her and her family from certain death. This is because Rahab had what I like to call a walking faith and not merely a talking faith. And Rahab's walking faith rescued her when the Israelites went walking around the Jericho wall. In Joshua 6, we read about it in verses 17 and 25 (NIV).

> The city and all that is in it are to be devoted to the Lord. Only Rahab the prostitute and all who are with her in her house shall be spared, because she hid the spies we sent.

> Joshua spared Rahab the prostitute, with her family and all who belonged to her, because she hid the men Joshua had sent as spies to Jericho—and she lives among the Israelites to this day.

In Joshua's command to the Israelites to march around Jericho according to the instruction of the Lord, he made sure that the Israelites knew to spare Rahab and everyone in her house. This *chesed* covered and protected not only Rahab but also everyone who gathered in her home. And it's not just a concept we read about in the Old Testament—it shows up in the New Testament as well. The apostle Paul writes to believers about the sanctification, or saving power in history, that a believer has when in the home with an unbeliever. "The unbelieving husband is sanctified through his wife, and the unbelieving wife is sanctified through her believing husband; for otherwise your children are unclean, but now they are holy" (1 Corinthians 7:14).

In this passage, to be sanctified does not mean to be saved from hell when you die. The Greek word *hagiazo* means to be "dedicated," "purified," and "set apart." God has arranged His covenantal covering so that simply being in the same family as one of His own will have its benefits. For Rahab's family, that meant their lives were saved when their entire community was annihilated.

Notice the way Rahab and her family were saved. We often overlook an important lesson in the text when we study the passage about the battle of Jericho. We all know how Israel defeated Jericho. The Israelites walked around the outer wall of the city once a day for six days. On the seventh day they walked around it seven times, blew their trumpets, and shouted. And as the song says, "the wall came a-tumblin' down." But in fact, it didn't just tumble. Joshua 6:20 tells us that "the wall collapsed." It fell flat. Jericho's ground zero was a disaster zone.

Except for one location.

Remember what we noticed at the beginning of our look at Rahab? Rahab had followed the first three rules for real estate: location, location, and location. She had chosen her location directly on the Jericho wall. Yet even though Rahab's house was built into the wall, as we saw earlier, and even though the walls of Jericho collapsed, Rahab's house remained intact. While everything else crumbled around them, Rahab and her family were safe. We know this because Joshua 2:18-19 specifically tells us that the spies told her to bring her family into her house. And in Joshua 6:17 we read that indeed Rahab and all who were with her in her house were spared.

There were two ways people died in Jericho on that day. Some died as a result of the collapse of the wall. Others died as a result of the Israelite army's attack. The spies had warned Rahab, "Anyone who goes out of the doors of your house and into the street, his blood will be on his own head, and we shall be free" (Joshua 2:19). But none of the soldiers could determine how the wall collapsed or whether any part of it remained intact. All they could do was walk around the wall. Nowhere does the text tell us that when they got to the part of the wall where Rahab lived, the army stopped walking and started tiptoeing. God told the Israelites His battle plan, they followed it, and God collapsed the wall, all the while keeping Rahab and everyone in her house completely safe.

We can trust God to do the same today. Even though things are collapsing all around you, when you have loved Him with His love language of faith, God's covenantal care can keep things together for you.

But in order for Rahab to witness the miracle on the wall, she had to go against her culture. She had to go against the crowd. When everyone else was buying into the philosophy of Jericho, Rahab set herself apart by hiding the spies.

It's clear that the citizens of Jericho had heard about the Israelites. Rahab told the spies that their reputation had brought fear into all those who had heard about them. It's just that no one else had the faith to act on what they feared. They knew the God of the Israelites had parted the Red Sea, but they had a wall. They knew the God of the Israelites had sent plagues on the Egyptians, but they had a wall. They knew the God of the Israelites had brought water from a rock, but they had a wall. Surely God couldn't do anything to their wall. "It's just not going to happen," they assumed. They were safe as long as they stayed away from the Israelites and inside the security of their wall.

But Rahab knew differently. She knew that a wall was no match for a God who can turn a sea into dry land. She knew that the only way that she and the members of her household were going to make it was to change sides—fast. The beauty of associating with God's kingdom and His purposes is that when stuff collapses all around you, God can still take care of you. Hebrews 12:28 refers to this as being part of an unshakable kingdom.

An amazing story of this happened at our church recently. Dallas, like every other city in the nation, was severely affected by the economic downturn in our country that began near the end of 2008. Companies closed. People lost their jobs. Homes were foreclosed upon. When the Dallas Independent School District (DISD) announced its largest job cut in its history—more than 1100 jobs were cut—I called for a special time of prayer at the beginning of both of our Sunday morning worship services. I wanted the church to specifically pray for anyone who might be affected by the cutbacks. More than 8000 people attend our worship services on a typical Sunday morning, and a large number of our members work for the DISD.

However, something extraordinary happened when I asked those to stand up who had either lost their job or were at threat to lose their job with the DISD. First it happened in our early service—no one stood up. I waited. I restated the request, making sure that everyone had heard me correctly. Still no one. So we prayed for those who were not members of our church who were affected by the cutbacks.

When second service started, I did the same thing. I made the same request—for the people who had lost their job or were at threat to lose their job by this, the largest cutback in DISD history, to stand. Again, no one stood up. Everyone remained seated. Not one single person stood. When I let the congregation know that no one had stood in first service either, the room burst into applause as we had just witnessed a modern-day Jericho-wall moment.

No, losing a job isn't the same as losing a life, as would have happened in Jericho on the day of battle. But God's covering was no less needed when jobs collapsed like broken-down walls in Dallas. Friend, if you will align yourself underneath God's kingdom agenda and His purposes, He can protect you wherever you are. He can take care of your house in a bad neighborhood. He can take care of your kids in a bad school. He can take care of your marriage in a culture that has redefined marriage and tries to get you to buy into their new definition. He can do this because God covers His friends. He has your back, even when it's up against a wall.

Your Past Doesn't Determine Your Future

But this book is not about God's protection, although that's important. It's about how God worked through people even when their decisions seemed to disqualify them. It's not about how to stay safe in the city of Jericho as much as it is about how God rewards faith regardless of who you are. This is exactly why I chose to include Rahab in our study—as an example of someone who probably thought her chances of being used by God were over long before any walls fell.

Rahab was a harlot. We've read that before. But God evidently wants us to remember her profession because no one else in the Bible is described with their title so frequently. We don't read "Moses the murderer" when the writers of the New Testament talk about faith. We don't read "Abraham the liar." We don't read "Noah the drunkard." But we do read "Rahab the harlot"—over and over again. Hebrews 11:31 and James 2:25 specifically refer to "Rahab the harlot." So why does God keep bringing up Rahab's title rather than leaving a sister alone? The answer is that God wants you and me to know through her example that our past does not have to determine our future.

Regardless of how wretched, twisted, or broken your past might be, it is not the sum total of your future. I don't know your past or how bad it is. I don't know how many men or how many women there were. I don't know if you were a hussy or a player. All I know is that the woman described in Joshua 2 is the same woman mentioned in Hebrews 11. The woman in Joshua 6 is also in James 2. In the Old Testament, we were introduced to her as a harlot, but in the New Testament, she is an example of righteousness, godliness, power, and victory because God can turn a mess into a miracle.

It doesn't get much messier than selling your body to man after man, stranger after stranger, day in and day out, week after month after year. That's about as messy as a life can get. But this messed-up harlot is in the Hall of Faith next to Moses, Abraham, and Sarah. Rahab's name is right there with Noah, Enoch, and Abel. She will forever be inscribed in a place of honor by the God of the universe even though she had no religious background or education and no spiritually devoted husband—just a shameful career. Regardless of all of that, when Rahab connected her purposes to God's purposes by faith, everything got turned around. What's more, it didn't just get turned around on paper to be recorded for history. It got turned around in her everyday life. Rahab didn't just end up with her name mentioned in the Bible as a great example of faith; Rahab got her life back.

Scripture is rich and complex. So much of it is intertwined, and if you don't read it all, you might miss something. Rahab shows up not only in James and Hebrews but also in Matthew. We learn that after the walls of Jericho fell and Rahab was saved, she was married and gave birth to a child who would end up in the lineage of our Savior. Matthew 1:5-6 (NIV) says, "Salmon the father of Boaz, whose mother was Rahab, Boaz the father of Obed, whose mother was Ruth, Obed the father of Jesse, and Jesse the father of King David." Rahab ends up being the great-great-grandmother to Israel's most highly esteemed king—King David—and forever linked to the lineage of the King of Kings, Jesus Christ.

When Rahab left Jericho, she left her profession behind. Instead of hanging out on the corner, she started hanging out with the people of God. As a result, God gave Rahab a family. Maybe Salmon was intrigued by her faith, or maybe he was impressed by her ability to outwit the emissaries in Jericho. Jewish tradition suggests that Rahab was a proselyte of great courage and that Salmon may have been one of the two spies she hid on the roof. Whatever it was that attracted Salmon to Rahab, we're told that he married the former call girl and turned her into a lady.

Rahab the hooker got herself a husband—a husband with a job. In fact, in 1 Chronicles 2:51, we read that Salmon was the "father of Bethlehem." The word for *father* in passages like this generally refers to a ruler or chief. Because of its positioning between similar verses relating to known place names rather than people, "Bethlehem" is understood to be a location in this passage, and not a person. So Rahab didn't just end up with any old Joe from the tribe of Judah. God hooked Rahab up with a ruler of the city that would one day be the birthplace of the Messiah.

Not only that, but as we've seen, God then gave Rahab a child, Boaz, who would have a child by Ruth named Obed, who would have a child named Jesse, who would have a baby named David. And David's line would flow through Mary's husband, Joseph, giving Jesus Christ the legal right to be the King of the Jews. Joseph wasn't Jesus' biological father, but his lineage gave Jesus the legal right to David's throne. And in the book of Luke, we're told that Mary was also a descendant of King David, and through her as well, Jesus received his biological right to the throne of David, qualifying Him twice to be the King of the Jews, as had been declared by the Word of God.

How is that for turning things around? How is that for taking a seemingly hopeless person in a hopeless land in a hopeless situation and honoring her faith with a hope that extends to everyone? Don't tell me that God can't turn your situation around. If He can do it for Rahab, He can do it for anyone.

I don't know about your past, but I doubt it could get much worse than Rahab's. And even if it is, that's not too hard for God to redeem if you will connect your life choices with His kingdom purposes. When you do that, God can rescue you from your collapsing environment and place you right where you need to be to make the connections you need to make for your future. Trust Him the way Rahab did. Fear Him the way Rahab did. Let Him know you trust and fear Him through your actions just as Rahab did. Remember, God's love language is faith. He longs to call you His friend, but He wants to know that you trust Him first.

The Scarlet Cord

Rahab trusted God and demonstrated her faith through her actions. In Joshua 2:17-18, 20-21 we read what Rahab was asked to do as a sign of her faith.

> The men said to her, "We shall be free from this oath to you which you have made us swear, unless, when we come into the land, you tie this cord of scarlet thread in the window through which you let us down, and gather to yourself into the house your father and your mother and your brothers and all your father's household...But if you tell this business of ours, then we shall be free from the oath which you have made us swear." She said, "According to your words, so be it." So she sent them away, and they departed; and she tied the scarlet cord in the window.

It's all about the scarlet cord. The men made it clear to Rahab that when the soldiers came, they wouldn't know who she was or where she lived. They would need a marker so they could identify and protect her and her family. What they chose was a scarlet cord. Scarlet is a color similar to red, and *cord* can be translated *ribbon*. As in Tony Orlando and Dawn's "Tie a Yellow Ribbon 'Round the Old Oak Tree," the purpose of the ribbon was to send a message. The yellow ribbon shouted, "This is your home, and you are welcome here!" Rahab's red ribbon sent a different message: "This is the home of the hooker who helped the spies, and it's not to be destroyed."

Why is it important that the cord is red? You've probably heard of red-light districts. In red-light districts, red lights designate houses of prostitution. In biblical culture, sex workers didn't have red lights, but they did have red ribbons to attach to their doors, signifying to travelers that theirs was a house of prostitution. The red ribbon, like a red light, identified the sin that took place in that house.

But in Rahab's case, the spies had her hang a scarlet cord in her window. This is the same window out of which the spies had escaped. When she hung a sign of her sin, an acknowledgment of who she was, in the place where she had chosen to demonstrate her faith, she received salvation.

When the Israelites were in Egypt at the time of the Passover, a similar thing occurred. God instructed them to put the blood of a lamb on their doorposts, and when the angel saw the red blood, he passed over their homes.

Friend, when Jesus Christ shed His blood for your sin and for my sin, His blood was offered as our salvation. When we acknowledge and confess our sin, displaying our faith in the blood of the Lamb, we are spared from the wrath and judgment that we so rightly deserve. God can pardon any sin. No sin is so great that Christ's blood cannot cover it.

Because of Jesus Christ and His blood, God can do for you what He did for Rahab and for Moses—if you will acknowledge your need for a Savior and follow Him as Lord. He will turn around a seemingly hopeless situation or hopeless life.

The scarlet cord acknowledges that you have messed up but that you are trusting God's grace to fix you up. It acknowledges that you have failed but that when you believe, He can redeem your failure. You were bad, but God can make you better. A terrible sinner can one day be a glorious saint because as God moves around, collapsing the sinful world that does not respond to Him, He sees the blood of Jesus Christ over you, passes by you, and gives you the deliverance you need, just as He did for Rahab. As we have seen with Rahab, regardless of how bad your yesterday is, it does not have to determine your tomorrow. God wrote a whole new chapter for her life and included her in the New Testament.

As He did with Rahab, He can do with you. God can start your life all over again.

Just tie your ribbon around Calvary.

I'm not saying you need to go tell everyone your business. But you do need to be honest with God—be real with Him and admit that you need Him to show you an extra measure of grace and mercy. Tell God that you need a new start. Maybe you've been used, abused, and messed over when all you were looking for was love and acceptance. Let God know that you're now looking to Him for love and acceptance—a love and acceptance that will not only rescue you from your today but also give you a brighter tomorrow.

God chose a murderer in Midian and used him to lead His people to freedom. He chose a harlot in Canaan and used her in one of the greatest Israelite victories of all time—and He even included her in the lineage of Christ. God is no respecter of persons. He is just waiting to hear you speak His love language of faith.

3

Jacob Was a Liar

Jacob was a liar. He tricked, connived, and deceived to get what he wanted and to go where he wanted to go. In fact, Jacob's name literally means "trickster," and he truly lived up to it.

Jacob could manipulate things to make them work out the way he wanted them to. He often schemed to force his own goals into being. One of those goals, as we see in Genesis, was to inherit the family blessing, the birthright that belonged to his older brother, Esau.

Yet because he wasn't the oldest son, Jacob resorted to conniving in order to trick his father, Isaac, into blessing him rather than Esau. With both the help and encouragement of his mother, Rebekah, Jacob dressed up like Esau, talked like Esau, smelled like Esau, acted like Esau, and even put wool on his hands and neck so that he would feel like Esau when touched.

Because of Isaac's age, his sensory perception—especially his vision—had diminished. Isaac couldn't be certain whether the son standing in front of him to receive the family blessing was Esau, the son who was supposed to receive it. He couldn't see clearly enough to distinguish who it was that stood before him. What concerned him was that the voice he heard sounded more like Jacob's than Esau's.

> Then Isaac said to Jacob, "Come near so I can touch you, my son, to know whether you really are my son Esau or not."
> Jacob went close to his father Isaac, who touched him and said, "The voice is the voice of Jacob, but the hands are the hands of Esau." He did not recognize him, for his hands were hairy like those of his brother Esau; so he proceeded to bless him. "Are you really my son Esau?" he asked.
> "I am," he replied (Genesis 27:21-24 NIV).

The account could have read, "'I am,' he *lied*," because Esau wasn't standing before Isaac. It was Jacob. Yet because Jacob lied, tricking his father, Isaac blessed him, all the while thinking he was actually Esau.

This wasn't the only time Jacob manipulated to get his own way. He had done it earlier with Esau himself. Scripture describes Esau as a manly man. He was a hunter, and according to Genesis 25:27 (NIV), a "man of the open country." Jacob, on the other hand, was a man who was "content to stay at home among the tents." However, one day when Esau came home from the open country, he found Jacob cooking a meal. Jacob, recognizing Esau's hunger, took advantage of the situation.

> Once when Jacob was cooking some stew, Esau came in from the open country, famished. He said to Jacob, "Quick, let me have some of that red stew! I'm famished!" (That is why he was also called Edom.)
> Jacob replied, "First sell me your birthright."
> "Look, I am about to die," Esau said. "What good is the birthright to me?"

But Jacob said, "Swear to me first." So he swore an oath to him, selling his birthright to Jacob.

Then Jacob gave Esau some bread and some lentil stew. He ate and drank, and then got up and left.

So Esau despised his birthright (Genesis 25:29-34 NIV).

Not only did Jacob trick his father, Isaac, out of Esau's birthright, he manipulated Esau out of it as well. Jacob made sure to cover all of his bases in his scheme to get what was not rightfully his. This is because the blessing Jacob sought was more than just warm wishes from a father to a son. It involved authority, security, prosperity, and power. Part of the blessing is recorded for us in Genesis 27:28-29 (NIV).

> May God give you heaven's dew
>   and earth's richness—
>   an abundance of grain and new wine.
> May nations serve you
>   and peoples bow down to you.
> Be lord over your brothers,
>   and may the sons of your mother bow
>   down to you.
> May those who curse you be cursed
>   and those who bless you be blessed.

In other words, the blessing meant that God was not only going to take care of Jacob's present but also secure his future. God was going to go ahead of Jacob and work things out for him so that at each place in his life, everything would be ready for him before he got there. When you receive a blessing, God arranges the situations in your life so that as you enter them, they are ready for you and you are ready for them. The problem was that Jacob received a blessing that his character was not ready to receive. Remember, Jacob is a trickster. He wanted a good thing, but he wasn't yet the kind of person who could handle the good thing when he got it.

Many of us today are in a similar situation. We desire God's blessings. We want all that God will provide, and yet we're not ready to handle all that God has in store for us should He give it. Maybe you know someone like that—or maybe you *are* someone like that.

It could be that your home life early on left an indelible scar on your soul that affects the way you perceive life and interact with others. Or maybe you hung out with the wrong crowd for too long, and their dysfunctions have become your dysfunctions. It could be that wrong thought patterns have created strongholds in your mind, affecting your choices, your actions, and even your own self-perception. You want what God has in store for you, but situations and people have made it difficult to respond correctly when He tries to give it to you. You doubt, fuss, complain, or fear being grateful because you think you may have to do something to earn it or to keep it, and you fear that the good that God has for you will leave as quickly as it came.

If that describes you, I want to encourage you to stay on the path that God has for you as He seeks to develop your character—just as He sought to develop Jacob's. You have a blessing. You have a right to your blessing. Unlike Jacob, you didn't need to trick anyone to get it. Your blessing has already been secured for you. In fact, you have every blessing you could ever need. As a believer in Jesus Christ, you have already inherited your blessing through the new covenant. Paul tells us in Ephesians 1:3 that God has "blessed us with every spiritual blessing in the heavenly places in Christ." However, it's possible to be blessed and not yet be experiencing your blessing because God is waiting until you're able to handle the blessing He has given to you.

God blessed Israel by delivering them from the oppression and illegitimate control of the Egyptians, but Israel took 40 years to arrive at their blessing in Canaan. The reason why it took the Israelites 40 years is that they first had to go through a process of development in the wilderness. The doubt that had kept them from entering the

Promised Land when they first arrived had to be removed from them. In other words, God wouldn't let them experience the fullness of His blessing until their character was ready to receive it and handle it the way it should be handled.

God interacts with us the same way. Oftentimes that means that God allows trials in our lives to prepare us for where He's taking us.

Trials hurt. They stretch us, bend us, twist us, and pressure us as they develop us into the people God would have us to be. A chef in an authentic pizzeria stretches the dough, pounds it, flattens it, rolls it, twirls it, and then cooks it. A pizza can't become all that a pizza was intended to be until the dough has gone through the necessary process of becoming all that it was made to be. Piling some sausage, sauce, onions, and tomatoes on top of a wad of dough will never make a pizza. Rather, the dough has to be worked before it can be the proper foundation all of the toppings and a delicious meal.

It's easy to want the goodness of God and the blessings of God, but God wants to make sure we're able to handle the power of God when it comes time for Him to give it. Many of us have a glorious future deposited in our account, but God is still walking us through our personal development so we don't waste that future when we get it. He wants to make sure we can handle the blessing He has in store for us before He delivers it to us.

Jacob may have tricked both Isaac and Esau to get God's blessing, but God knew Jacob wasn't ready to receive that blessing even though it was now his. God knew that Jacob was still being too true to his name—a trickster. He was still too full of himself to benefit from the blessing should God have given it to him right away. Rather, God wanted to be certain that Jacob was ready for everything that He had in store so that when He gave it, it wouldn't be wasted.

Fleeing Because of Sin

Immediately after Isaac gave the blessing to Jacob, Jacob had to flee. Esau was angry because of what Jacob had done and had even threatened to kill him. So Rebekah convinced Isaac to send Jacob away by telling Isaac she didn't want their son to marry one of the Hittite women living around them. The Hittite women had previously caused Isaac and Rebekah a tremendous amount of grief, and because of that, Rebekah was able to persuade Isaac to send Jacob to his uncle Laban's home in the region where she had come from.

At Isaac's urging, Jacob took off for Haran. Yet on the way there, God spoke to him in a dream in which he saw a stairway reaching into heaven.

> I am the LORD, the God of your father Abraham and the God of Isaac. I will give you and your descendants the land on which you are lying. Your descendants will be like the dust of the earth, and you will spread out to the west and to the east, to the north and to the south. All peoples on earth will be blessed through you and your offspring. I am with you and will watch over you wherever you go, and I will bring you back to this land. I will not leave you until I have done what I have promised you (Genesis 28:13-15 NIV).

Once again, Jacob received the promise of a blessing. Yet just as before, Jacob wasn't ready to receive the blessing itself. God told him He would bring him back to the land He had promised him. But before that could happen, a few other things had to happen. One of the first things was that Jacob needed to get a taste of his own medicine and learn how it felt to be tricked. This lesson came about when he fell in love with Rachel, one of his uncle's daughters.

A Tale of Two Daughters

Laban had two daughters. The oldest was Leah, and the younger was Rachel. Scripture tells us that Jacob loved Rachel. In fact, it might be safe to conclude that Jacob loved Rachel at first sight. We read in Genesis 29:11 that the first time Jacob saw Rachel, he kissed her and began to weep aloud. The text gives us a hint about one of the reasons why. It says in verse 17, "Rachel had a lovely figure and was beautiful." Apparently this girl had it going on so much that she was able to make a grown man cry.

However, local cultural tradition required that the older sister marry before the younger. As we have seen, Jacob wasn't a fan of following cultural traditions or honoring the way things were supposed to be. When he first met Rachel at the well after having traveled a long distance, Jacob chose to disregard the rules that governed the use of the well. In Genesis 29:7-10 we read that Jacob rolled the stone away to water Rachel's sheep before the normal time had come for watering the sheep. The greeting Jacob gave to Rachel that day, as well, was different from the way the local people normally did things. Kissing a girl and weeping on a first meeting wasn't the social norm.

Seeing himself as a person who didn't have to operate according to the rules of culture, Jacob asked Laban for Rachel instead of Leah. Yet because Jacob had tricked his father, Isaac, out of Esau's birthright, Jacob had to flee empty-handed from his homeland. He was in no position to offer the customary bride-price for Rachel so that he could marry her immediately. Instead, Jacob had to work for seven years before Laban would give him his daughter in marriage.

Genesis 29:20 tells us that the seven years Jacob worked for Rachel "seemed to him but a few days because of his love for her." Yet on the night Jacob was supposed to marry his heart's (or his eyes') desire, Laban pulled a "Jacob" on him. Laban tricked Jacob by giving him his older daughter, Leah, instead. Apparently caught up in the celebration of the event, Jacob didn't even notice he had married Leah until the next morning. Maybe he had participated too heavily in the celebration leading up to the wedding. Who knows? But what we do know is that "when morning came, there was Leah! So Jacob said to

Laban, 'What is this you have done to me? I served you for Rachel, didn't I? Why have you deceived me?'" (Genesis 29:25 NIV).

The tables had turned. Now Jacob was the one being tricked. A perfect example of poetic irony had just played out because, as the verse says, Jacob the deceiver actually asked Laban, "Why have you deceived me?"

Laban replied, "It is not our custom here to give the younger daughter in marriage before the older one" (verse 26 NIV). Once again, we're dealing with the entitlement of the older versus the entitlement of the younger. Earlier, Jacob had deceived Isaac to get what the oldest son should have gotten. Now, Laban deceives Jacob to give him what his oldest daughter should be given. The saying, "What goes around comes around" may have been conceived in Haran.

Regardless, Jacob made another deal to serve Laban for another seven years in order to marry the woman who had captured him, Rachel. Jacob married Rachel immediately following the completion of Leah's bridal week and then went on to serve his second set of seven years. We read that Jacob "made love to Rachel also, and his love for Rachel was greater than his love for Leah" (Genesis 29:30 NIV).

The Long Night

During that time and the years after, Jacob acquired a large amount of wealth. Just as God had promised, He blessed him. We read not only that Jacob's wives provided him with numerous sons and daughters but also that God blessed Jacob's property. Genesis 30:43 (NIV) tells us, "In this way the man grew exceedingly prosperous and came to own large flocks, and female and male servants, and camels and donkeys."

After 20 years of acquiring a significant amount of wealth and security, Jacob decided it was time to return home. Uncertain of how Esau would treat him upon his return, Jacob proceeded slowly in his travels with his wives, children, and property. Sending messengers ahead of him to let Esau know of his return, Jacob received frightening news when the messengers returned: Esau was coming to meet him—and he was bringing 400 men.

In Jacob's mind, there was only one reason why his brother would be coming to meet him with an escort of 400 men. Esau's rage must not have subsided, and he was surely coming to kill Jacob, his wives, and his children. "In great fear and distress Jacob divided the people who were with him into two groups, and the flocks and herds and camels as well. He thought, 'If Esau comes and attacks one group, the group that is left may escape'" (Genesis 32:7-8 NIV).

Jacob went to great lengths to protect his family and his possessions from Esau. He sent ahead a peace offering, hoping to appease Esau. He prayed to God, reminding Him of the promise of blessing He had given him. He sent his wives, children, and possessions across the ford of Jabbok, where they would be safe. And then, after all of his planning and praying, Jacob was left alone.

It was at this time that God met with Jacob once again. Twenty years had passed since God had first appeared to Jacob in a dream at Bethel, showing him a stairway into heaven and telling him of His promise to bless him. Now, 20 years later, God returns to meet Jacob at the Jabbok to see if Jacob's character has developed enough to receive the fruition of that blessing. God will frequently reveal our character by putting us in situations that allow us to feel afraid, frustrated, defeated, or lonely. This is exactly what He did with Jacob.

Jacob was alone that night. We read that he was in "great fear and distress." He was blessed with wives, children, and possessions, but he was a blessed man on the run, unable to enjoy what God had given him. One reason why Jacob was a man on the run is that Jacob had defined manhood the wrong way. Jacob thought that to be a man meant being able to fool people into giving him what he wanted. He thought that being a man was all wrapped up in his swagger—the way he walked, talked, or carried himself. Jacob hadn't yet learned what a real man was, and he wasn't about to learn until God put him in a situation that he couldn't trick, connive, or deceive his way out of.

Esau approaches Jacob with 400 men—an entire army. And Jacob is alone. Already afraid of the upcoming battle with his brother, Jacob finds himself in an unexpected battle that night. "So Jacob was left alone, and a man wrestled with him till daybreak" (Genesis 32:24 NIV).

Somebody had come out of nowhere and started wrestling Jacob, trying to pin him to the mat. Just as Hulk Hogan made a surprise appearance on *American Idol*, this person had appeared out of nowhere. We suddenly have WrestleMania all night long. Keep in mind that this is the Jacob who didn't even like to go out into the "open country"—perhaps because he didn't want to risk getting his hands dirty. This is the Jacob who once preferred to stay "close to the tents." This is the Jacob who would scheme and trick to get his way or to get out of a situation that he didn't want to be in.

And now this same Jacob is wrestling with an oversized enemy all night long. You would think he might start whining and cry uncle, but he won't quit. Jacob won't throw in the towel. With his back up against the wall, Jacob refused to back down. He fought for his family. He fought for his future. He fought for the promise of the blessing God had given him. In fact, he fought so hard and for so long that "when the man saw that he could not overpower him, he touched the socket of Jacob's hip so that his hip was wrenched" (Genesis 32:25 NIV). The opponent must have been impressed with Jacob when he saw that he could not overpower him.

Here we have Jacob running for his life from Esau. While running for his life, another man shows up at night, grabs him, and will not let him go. More than that, he injures him deeply. By touching his hip, he dislocates it—pushing it out of joint. Jacob is already tired and frightened while he's fighting, but to make matters worse, now he is in pain as well.

What does this have to do with the full realization of Jacob's blessing? Everything. That night, Jacob experienced the same thing many of us experience before living out the fullness of God's blessings—brokenness. We are broken when God strips us of our self-sufficiency, when we cannot use our wit, intellect, charm, money, power, or influence to make something happen on our own. We are broken when God shows up and reveals that we're not enough on our own.

God will often allow us to be put in a situation we cannot fix so we will discover that He is the only one who can fix it. Jacob is wrestling in a desperate situation. He is in pain and anguish, and his strength is spent in an all-night battle that isn't even the fight he was anticipating.

But something happened during this fight that forever changed Jacob. In the middle of his pain, defeat, and hopelessness, Jacob discovered that this fight wasn't about the fight itself. This battle was about much more than just two individuals seeing who could last the longest. As Jacob wrestled all night long, he learned that this fight had to do with his blessing. Somewhere in the process of dislocation, being broken, and having been reduced in a painful situation that he could not fix, Jacob discovered a connection between his pain and God's purposes.

The opponent eventually said to Jacob, "Let me go, for it is daybreak."

"I will not let you go unless you bless me," Jacob answered (Genesis 32:26 NIV).

Jacob recognized the connection between his problem and God's blessing. Realizing that he was in a lose-lose situation—wrestling a man who had the power to dislocate his hip simply by touching it, and going up against a vengeful brother with an army of 400 men the next day—Jacob knew that the only way he was going to get what he wanted this time was for God to give it to him. He couldn't trick his way into experiencing this blessing. He couldn't manipulate his way into an inheritance. He couldn't even work his way into achieving and living out the life he wanted. Jacob had ultimately discovered that if it was going to be done—if his blessing was going to be fulfilled—it would be God, and God alone, who would do it.

One of the problems we often face as believers is mistaking the hand of man for the hand of God. We frequently fail to make the connection between our pain and God's purposes. We need to realize that there is often more going on than just having a bad day or working with a difficult person. God often uses painful situations to shape our character so we will become strong enough to handle the blessing when He gives it. He wants to make sure that what He gives us will not be wasted on weak faith.

Jacob had already been blessed. He just hadn't experienced the fullness of that blessing being lived out. Jacob had what many of us have—a blessing on paper. The Bible is full of blessings on paper. Thousands of blessings are promised to us in the Bible. But there comes a time in each of our lives—just as it did with Jacob—when we need more than a blessing on paper. We need God to lift that blessing right off the paper and bring it to life.

But God oftentimes won't bring the blessing into our experience until our character has been made ready to receive it. So God's challenge can be to get men and women to wrestle with Him. We will wrestle with other men and women. We will even wrestle with ourselves. But we often won't wrestle with God in the midst of our pain. We blame others, whine, or complain rather than wrestle with God in order to discover the blessing He has promised us. Wrestling with men may change something in history, but wrestling with God can change things for eternity.

Wrestling with God radically changed Jacob, as is revealed to us in his name. "The man asked him, 'What is your name?'

"'Jacob,' he answered" (Genesis 32:27 NIV).

Now to me, this seems like a weird conversation to be having during a fight. Can you imagine yourself wrestling and struggling and groaning with someone and then having them say, "By the way, what is your name?" You're trading punches, and all of a sudden the other person asks you your name. Strange. However, when we consider the significance of names in this time and culture, it makes perfect sense. In the Bible, a name was never just about the name. A name revealed a person's identity, character, and purpose.

Jacob was asked his name because it reflected the methodology Jacob had always used to get what he wanted. He was a trickster. Jacob relied on himself to go where he wanted to go and to accomplish what he wanted to accomplish. But in order to receive the fullness of his blessing, Jacob had to be broken first. Jacob had to let go of his self-reliance. He had to change his name.

In Genesis 32:28 (NIV) we read, "Then the man said, 'Your name will no longer be Jacob, but Israel, because you have struggled with God and with humans and have overcome.'" Jacob's name would no longer be Trickster because Jacob was no longer functioning in that mode. Jacob was to be called Israel because he struggled with God and with man and he had the strength of character and faith to hang in there and overcome. Jacob's new point of reference was to be that very moment. And it would define him for the rest of his life.

The problem with many of us is that we're living under the wrong name. We have a generation of people who are relating to the wrong name. For example, we have musical artists calling girls all sorts of names that should not define them. And even worse, we see the girls dancing and singing along with these wrong labels. They are essentially being called tramps—and they're going along with it. They have adopted a name given to them by a culture that tries to define them.

One reason they have responded to these names is that they haven't heard anyone giving them the right name. One reason they've never heard the right name is that we have a generation of men who are living with their own wrong names themselves. It's hard to give somebody a name when you aren't even sure what your own name is.

Jacob got a new name the night he wrestled with God. Yet what's interesting about that night is how Jacob discovered that the opponent who was trying to pin him to the ground was actually God trying to lift him up. The challenger he thought was trying to work against him was actually God working things out for him. In order for God to move Jacob to the point where he would relinquish his name, he had to break him. He had to break the hold that his name had on him. He had to replace his history, background, and identity with something new.

The Name of God

When Jacob understood his new name, he asked, "Please tell me your name." But Jacob didn't get the answer he expected. Instead, he heard the rhetorical question, "Why is it that you ask my name?" (Genesis 32:29).

But Jacob didn't need an answer to his question. He already had it. Jacob had just been given his new name, Israel. He was also told why he was given that name: "because you have struggled with God."

In other words, all Jacob needed to know was who *he* was. If he knew who *he* was, then he knew whom he was wrestling with. In my Tony Evans paraphrase, the response to Jacob's question was simply this: "I just told you your name—Israel. Israel means you struggled with God. In order to know my name, all you have to do is know your name. Because my name is in the name I just gave you. All you have to do is continue to tell yourself who you are, and as you do, you will know who I am because I have shared my name with you."

By fully identifying himself with his new name, Israel—which meant that he had struggled with God and won—Jacob would always remember who his opponent had been that night. The answer to his question was within his own name.

We read in Genesis 32:29 that after Jacob realized whom he had wrestled, God blessed him there just as He had promised. Jacob got his blessing from God. "So Jacob called the place Peniel, saying, 'It is because I saw God face to face, and yet my life was spared'" (verse 30 NIV).

In other words, Jacob knew at that point that he had not actually overcome or prevailed against the one he wrestled. Rather, he was spared. Just as a father who is playing basketball with his son will sometimes let his son score against him because he is trying to develop him, teach him, direct him, and train him, God will oftentimes allow us to prevail in our struggles with Him in order to teach us something. God demonstrated His power by dislocating Jacob's hip. He could have dislocated his heart just as quickly. But God let Jacob live through his struggle because in it and through it, He taught him where his true blessing lies—in Him. The wrestling match ended with the sun rising above Jacob and him "limping because of his hip" (verse 31 NIV).

For the rest of Jacob's life, his limp served as a constant reminder of that night. It was a reminder that every time he moved, he couldn't make it on his own. Jacob could never take one step again without remembering that God had spared him. Jacob was blessed, but his limp reminded him that it was God alone who had blessed him.

Which leads me to a question: Do you want to be a blessed person with a limp, or do you want to be just another person who can keep on walking without a problem? God will let you go through life with your blessing still on paper and your hip feeling just fine. He will let you think you're calling the shots and determining how things turn out. But if you truly want to be blessed, at times it's going to require a limp or two. It's when God breaks us and strips us of our self-reliance that we are free to see Him face-to-face.

Not only that, but when we take our eyes off ourselves, we learn to recognize God's blessings and understand whom they are intended to reach. A blessing is never meant for you alone. A blessing is always intended to continue through you to someone else. In the book of Hebrews, we witness Jacob passing the blessing that he had received to his grandsons. He gave them a legacy of God's faithfulness, protection, and provision. We read in Hebrews 11:21, "By faith Jacob, as he was dying, blessed each of the sons of Joseph, and worshiped, leaning on the top of his staff." Obviously still bothered by his hip, Jacob leaned on his staff and transferred the blessing of divine favor to his grandsons. A blessing is a biblical blessing only when it can extend through you to others. In this case, the trickster ended up in the Hall of Faith because he learned how to view his blessing as God views it.

In fact, because Jacob learned how to view his blessing as God views it, he made a surprising decision at his death. We read that Jacob was asked to be buried with Leah rather than with Rachel (Genesis 49:29-32). He did this even though he clearly loved Rachel more than he loved Leah. The Scripture made the point of Jacob's love for Rachel clear in many places. Even in his old age Jacob spoke of Rachel in terms of great endearment. He said, "As I was returning from Paddan, to my sorrow Rachel died in the land of Canaan while we were still on the way" (Genesis 48:7 NIV). Yet because Jacob now viewed his blessing through God's eyes as it was meant for others, Jacob requested to be buried with Leah. After all, it was Leah who gave birth to Judah, who would become the father of David and in the line of Jesus Christ. It was Leah who was going to be used in the messianic line. It was Leah who gave birth to Levi, the forerunner of the tribe especially chosen to serve God in His temple. When Jacob positioned himself underneath God's overarching rule and perspective, he then connected himself with Leah, the wife who had been unloved.

An interesting thing to note about Leah is the names she gave her four sons. Desperately hoping for a love connection with her husband, Leah chose to give her sons names that reflected her heart for him. Her first son's name, Reuben, literally means "look" and "son." In other words, Leah was saying to Jacob, "Look at me, I have given you a son." Leah's second son was named Simeon, meaning "the Lord hears." Leah said that because the Lord heard that she was hated by her husband, and He blessed her with a son.

Leah's third son was named Levi, which literally means "to attach or connect." Once again, Leah expressed her deep need to be loved by her husband through her son's name. However, by the time Leah had given birth to her fourth son, she had learned, as Jacob would later, that a true blessing only comes from God. She named him Judah, which means "praise." As a result, in death, Leah received the honor of having her husband by her side—an honor she never experienced in her life.

Both Jacob and Leah leave a legacy of faith, reminding each of us that it's never too late for God to take whatever situation or mess you might find yourself in and turn it around for His purposes and glory. If you will humble yourself in His presence, accepting the brokenness that often accompanies humility, He can bless you greatly and take you straight to your destiny.

I took a flight recently from Raleigh, North Carolina, back to Dallas, where I live. As we were approaching Dallas, the captain came on the loudspeaker and let us know that there were a number of storm clouds around the Dallas–Fort Worth airport and that the airport had temporarily shut down. As a result, we couldn't land. So instead, the captain flew our plane to Abilene.

While sitting on the tarmac in Abilene, waiting for the storms in Dallas to subside, I noticed a passenger get up and start collecting her bags out of the overhead compartment. Making her way up to the flight attendant, I overheard her say, "I was supposed to take a connecting flight from Dallas to Abilene. But since we are already in Abilene, I wanted to know if you would let me off here."

The flight attendant readily agreed and let the lady off the airplane. It wasn't the route she thought she was going to take to get to her location, but she had made it to her location anyhow. Friend, God is so good that He can take advantage of a diversion caused by turbulence in life that you might think has taken you off course for 20 years (as it did for Jacob). God can still take you right where you need to go.

You may think you've lost too many years due to a bad decision. Jacob had lost a few years of his own, as did Moses, whom we looked at earlier. But God can still get you where you need to go. It's never too late with God. He can turn a mess into a miracle—if you will simply realize that God is in control. You don't need to try to maneuver your way anywhere. Let Him direct you, bless you, and possibly even break you—so that He can rename you according to His perfect plan.

4

Jonah Was a Rebel

Jonah was a rebel. But he was also a prophet. James Dean might be forever remembered as the rebel without a cause, but Jonah was the rebel *with* a cause. Yet because of this, we witness a constant inner (and at times, outer) turmoil for Jonah throughout the events recorded about his life.

Scripture doesn't tell us much about Jonah. Only four short chapters give us a glimpse of this man. Because these chapters are tucked away between Obadiah and Micah, you're going to have to be intentional if you're going to read about Jonah. Though he doesn't get much airtime in the Bible, what he does get is packed with all the elements of an epic.

Our look at Jonah begins with a mission. It could fall into the category of a mission impossible, should Jonah choose to accept it. Which he doesn't. Instead, he chooses desertion, rebellion, and deception. After that, we find our rebel in the middle of a perfect storm while also being the target of an attempted murder—an attempted murder with a good cause, of course. Next, a life-saving whale appears, leading to repentance, rededication, and obedience. But then we see regret and a suicidal level of depression.

Jonah's story is both an epic failure and an epic success. His is a drama unlike many others yet with life principles applicable to all of us who have experienced personal failure, spiritual rebellion, anger, hate, cowardice, or just plain apathy.

Jonah Runs Away

The story begins with Jonah receiving his assignment from God. "The word of the LORD came to Jonah the son of Amittai saying, 'Arise, go to Nineveh the great city and cry against it, for their wickedness has come up before Me'" (Jonah 1:1-2).

Nineveh was the capital city of the Assyrian Empire. Known for its brutality and oppression (see Nahum 1), Assyria's conquests confirmed its reputation as a nation without mercy or compassion. In fact, the Assyrian armies tortured their enemies, sometimes skinning them alive and nailing their skins to a wall as a warning to others who might stand in their way. The Assyrians were a threat and an enemy to the Israelites in particular. Thus, Jonah may have hated the Assyrians as well as feared them. We may not know Jonah's exact feelings toward the Assyrians, but we do know that he refused his assignment from God to take a message of repentance to them.

> But Jonah rose up to flee to Tarshish from the presence of the LORD. So he went down to Joppa, found a ship which was going to Tarshish, paid the fare and went down into it to go with them to Tarshish from the presence of the LORD (Jonah 1:3).

Here we have a situation where Jonah intentionally places his relationship and fellowship with God beneath his hatred, fear, disdain, and contempt of the Assyrians. Twice this verse says that Jonah fled from the presence of the Lord.

Jonah knew that God was a gracious God, which meant that He could very well show mercy to the Ninevites. Rather than stick around to see that happen (or worse, even help make it happen), Jonah decided to run away from God's presence.

Jonah was a prophet who was fully aware of the omnipresence of God, so where did he think he was going? Maybe he wasn't sure. Yet he ran, just as many of us do from time to time. We think that if we stop talking to God or stop going to church, He no longer keeps up with our lives or what we're doing. Perhaps in periods of rebellion or spiritual distance, we too assume that we've left God's presence. But God is always near; He's aware of each of us every moment. God sees everything, and because of that, there's no place we can hide from Him. As the psalmist David wrote, God is acutely aware of where each of us is.

> O LORD, You have searched me and known me.
> You know when I sit down and when I rise up;
> > You understand my thought from afar.
> You scrutinize my path and my lying down,
> > And are intimately acquainted with all my ways...
> You have enclosed me behind and before,
> > And laid Your hand upon me...
> Where can I go from Your Spirit?
> > Or where can I flee from Your presence?
> If I ascend to heaven, You are there;
> > If I make my bed in Sheol, behold, You are there.
> If I take the wings of the dawn,
> > If I dwell in the remotest part of the sea,
> Even there Your hand will lead me,
> > And Your right hand will lay hold of me
> > (Psalm 139:1-3,5,7-10).

Even so, somehow Jonah had convinced himself that he could flee from God's presence. So that is what he set out to do.

Here we have a man who didn't like God's instructions. He wasn't happy about God's assignment at all. In fact, Jonah may have thought God had lost His mind. "Preach repentance to the Assyrians, God? You've got to be kidding. Not them—anyone but them!"

After all, the entire book of Nahum tells us that judgment and doom are coming to the Assyrians because of their wickedness. They were merciless warriors who boasted of their lust for blood. They recorded in their annals the annihilation of young and old alike.

However, at the time of Jonah, the Assyrian Empire was experiencing a period of vulnerability. Following the death of King Adad-nirari III in 783 BC, the nation went through a 37-year period of struggling to defend itself from its neighbors to the north. This is the setting in which God gave His instruction to Jonah.

This national situation for Nineveh produced two effects. One, it may have made Jonah less likely to want to preach repentance to a nation who might respond and avoid God's judgment but then go on years later to ultimately defeat the Israelites. Two, it may have made the Ninevites more open to answering a call for repentance in order to hold back God's wrath during a weaker time in their national defense.

It wasn't so much about God sending Jonah to Nineveh that upset this rebel prophet. Rather, it was *why* He told him to go and when. If God had sent Jonah to Nineveh to preach judgment, that would have been a different story. Jonah would have climbed aboard the first camel and delivered the message in record time. But to go to a brutal enemy who is experiencing a time of national weakness and tell them that God is going to give them a second chance before He destroys them—that's a completely different request. In Jonah's mind, these people didn't deserve a second chance. Not only that, but if they did get spared, they could get stronger and eventually attack the Israelites again.

So in order to help prevent what he did not want to come about, Jonah fled in the opposite direction. He didn't just stroll off. The passage clearly says that Jonah "rose up to flee." I'll make it plain—Jonah sprinted in the opposite direction. The prophet made a mad dash away from his Boss. I'm not sure Jonah believed he was running away from God as much as he was running away from God's expectations, demands, and requirements. "Get someone else to do this job, God," Jonah may have mumbled while boarding a ship in the opposite direction. "Not me!"

Keep in mind that Nineveh is approximately 550 miles by land from where Jonah was when God told him to go. But Jonah set sail for Tarshish, which is 2500 miles in the opposite direction by sea. Apparently, Jonah would rather sail 2500 miles away from the will of God than ride and walk 550 miles toward it. By making this choice, Jonah didn't just say no. Jonah shouted, "No way!" And to make sure his "no way" was clearly understood, he went in the other direction. Perhaps he thought that even when God did find him, it would be too late for Jonah to preach to the Ninevites.

Have you ever felt that way? Have you ever known what God wanted you to do but not been happy about it? Maybe you even had good, well-thought-out reasons why you didn't want to do what God had asked you to do. Too much unnecessary risk was involved, or you couldn't forgive that person He was asking you to forgive. So instead of simply telling God no, you made sure it was a firm "No way!"

Sometimes I've seen people who stop going to church, stop reading God's Word, or stop hanging out with people who have a close relationship with God because they don't want to be reminded of what God has said. They don't want to remember God's divine expectation, so they try to leave His presence. The problem with that strategy, though, is what I said earlier—God doesn't just hang out at church. As the psalmist tells us, "The earth is the LORD's, and all it contains, the world, and those who dwell in it" (Psalm 24:1). There is no place in God's creation where you can hide from Him. God has a personal GPS for each of us with our name on it. He can track us down wherever we are, just as He did with Jonah.

Not only can we not run away from God's presence, but when

we try, we always end up going *down*. It's never a step up. Just as Jonah went down to Joppa and went down into the ship, down is the only direction to go from God.

If you think by running from God, you're headed somewhere good, think again. You're really headed in a downward spiral even though it may not be immediately evident. Everything may look fine at first. When Jonah boarded the ship, he may have seen the seagulls, felt the warm breeze off the water, and gotten a bite to eat. His probably seemed like any other excursion out to sea. But what Jonah didn't know was that he was sailing straight into the heart of a storm that had his name written all over it. And a storm that has your name written on it doesn't simply subside with time. That storm lasts until it has accomplished its purpose.

In addition to going down when he ran from God's presence, Jonah also paid the fare. He had to pay for his ticket. This is because whenever you run from God, you have to pick up the tab. When you go in the opposite direction from where God wants to take you, you have to pay for the trip. The reverse of that is true as well. When you are in God's will, even if you don't want to be in God's will, He will pick up the tab. It's similar to when a company sends an employee on a trip. When it does, it takes responsibility for paying the fare. However, when the employee decides to go on a vacation, he or she has to pay for the airfare, hotel, food, and everything else involved.

The center of God's will is the safest place to be, and you can be assured that God is going to cover all your needs there as well. That's what He did with Jochebed, Moses' mother, when she put Moses in the Nile River to escape the wrath of the Egyptians. When Jochebed did as God had led her to do, Miriam, Moses' sister, came back from the Nile and told her that Pharaoh's daughter had taken Moses to raise him as her own and that she needed a nursemaid to help with him. Jochebed applied for the job and ended up getting paid to raise her own son (Exodus 2:9).

She got paid to raise her own son because when you're in the will of God, God picks up the tab. However, if you want to try things on your own, like Jonah, you will need to pay for it yourself. Running from God costs you. Always. It costs you money, time, health, progress, joy, mental stability, and especially peace.

Running from God cost Jonah all of that and more. Before he knew it, Jonah found himself on a ship in the middle of a perfect storm. We read, "The LORD hurled a great wind on the sea and there was a great storm on the sea so that the ship was about to break up" (Jonah 1:4).

Jonah made his decision. Then God made His.

Jonah said, "God, I'm running from You."

God said, "Jonah, I'm hurling a storm at you."

Jonah said, "God, I'm going in the other direction."

God said, "Jonah, I'm already there."

God then hurled a supersized wind straight at Jonah because God loved Jonah. He does the same for you and me when we need it too. Hebrews 12:6 tells us clearly that God disciplines those He loves.

One of the greatest assurances of God's love for you is that when you do rebel, He will not leave you alone. Rather, God will create a storm with your name on it, just as He did with Jonah. Jonah found himself in the midst of a storm because he had chosen to run from a God who loved him greatly.

If you're a son or daughter of God and are in rebellion against Him, expect bad weather. God loves you too much not to come after you. The circumstances in your life may get shaky if you have gone the opposite direction from where God wants you to go. But if you are in that situation, be assured that God is only trying to bring you back to where you should have been all along—in His presence and in His will.

Throwing the Prophet Overboard

We read in the first chapter of Jonah that when the sailors saw that

IT'S NOT TOO LATE

the ship was about to break up because of the storm, they "became afraid." Professional, rugged seamen suddenly became terrified of the enormous storm that God had hurled at Jonah. We know they became terrified because they did the unthinkable. These men, who made their living from transporting cargo from Joppa to Tarshish and back, decided to throw their livelihood overboard. We read in Jonah 1:5 that "they threw the cargo which was in the ship into the sea to lighten it for them." Translation: They threw their money away.

These sailors tossed their paycheck into the sea because of the violent storm. By that time, the sailors had decided they would do anything that needed to be done in order to simply survive. Jonah's rebellion was no longer affecting him alone. Now it was affecting the sailors on the ship and their families because these men—if they survived—would not get a paycheck this month. Children were going to go hungry because of Jonah. But judging from Jonah's response to the situation, he didn't care. In the middle of the disastrous storm, Jonah slept. We read, "But Jonah had gone below into the hold of the ship, lain down and fallen sound asleep."

Once again, fleeing from God's will had taken Jonah *down*, this time into the hold of the ship. Question: How does a person fall asleep on a ship that's about to break into a million pieces because of a storm? The answer is that Jonah had gotten so far outside of God's will that even when the storm hit, Jonah didn't recognize his name written all over it. Instead, he snored. Jonah's flight from God had taken him so far down—so low—that he lost touch with God Himself. Jonah had hit the snooze button on God's storm.

Yet while Jonah slept, the rest of the crew tried to figure out how to get out of the storm alive. Each of them had already cried out to his own god. Now they wanted Jonah to cry out to his as well. The captain located Jonah down in the hold and confronted him. "How is it that you are sleeping? Get up, call on your god. Perhaps your god will be concerned about us so that we will not perish" (Jonah 1:6).

If you read that too quickly, you might miss the significance of it.

The captain is an unbeliever. Jonah is a preacher. Here we have the unbeliever telling the preacher to pray. He is saying, "Preacher man, would you mind praying right now? Don't you think that might be a good idea?" Which just goes to show that a person can get so far out of the will of God that it takes sinners to get him to act like a saint. The passage doesn't tell us whether Jonah responded to the request or ran from that one as well. All we know is that soon after that, the crew said, "Come, let us cast lots so we may learn on whose account this calamity has struck us" (verse 7).

The crewmen understood that the storm they were facing was a spiritual problem, not just a meteorological one. Because of this, they decided to get to the bottom of it and find out who was causing the storm that was tearing their ship apart. As you might have guessed, the lot fell to Jonah. The crew demanded an explanation, so Jonah confessed, "I am a Hebrew, and I fear the LORD God of heaven who made the sea and the dry land" (verse 9).

Next, "the men became extremely frightened and they said to him, 'How could you do this?' For the men knew that he was fleeing from the presence of the LORD, because he had told them" (verse 10). Running from God had now created a messy situation for more than just Jonah, and understandably, the crewmen wanted to know how to stop the storm. Jonah told them that there was only one thing to do at this point. They needed to pick him up and toss him into the heart of the storm. If they would do this, Jonah told them, the sea would become calm again.

Jonah wasn't just trying to stop the storm with that suggestion. Jonah was choosing to die rather than to go to Nineveh. Of course he hadn't anticipated that a great fish was going to rescue him. As far as Jonah knew, when the sailors threw him into the sea, that was the curtain call for Jonah. He had gotten so far out of God's will that he was willing to commit suicide rather than do what God had asked him to do. Jonah didn't tell the sailors to turn the boat around and take him back to land so he could obey God. He told them to throw him into the sea. In fact, Jonah was much more eager to die than the men were to kill him. Rather than throw him overboard, the men "rowed desperately to return to land but they could not, for the sea was becoming even stormier against them" (verse 13). The more the sailors rowed, the more the winds howled. The sinners were trying to save the saint while the saint was intent on carrying out his own death wish.

Eventually the sailors gave up. They called on God for forgiveness for throwing Jonah overboard. Then they picked Jonah up and tossed him into the raging sea. And just as Jonah had told them it would, "the sea stopped its raging" (verse 15).

Seeing God's power revealed in the calming of the sea, the sailors feared Him and made sacrifices and vows to Him. Get this— the sailors who had been praying to false gods are now praying to Jonah's God. Jonah had led the men to salvation without even trying. This shows us an important principle about God: Even in our rebellion, God will still accomplish His work.

In the Belly of a Whale

Next we find Jonah gurgling in the water, about to be swallowed by a fish. Our rebel spends the next three days and nights in the stomach of that fish. Just when we thought Jonah couldn't go any farther down, he's gone even lower. Finally, there in the belly of that big fish, Jonah realizes he can't run from God any longer.

So far, the text hasn't indicated that he prayed. When the storm hit, the text never says that Jonah prayed. Even when the sailors asked Jonah to pray, we have no record that he actually did. Yet locked up inside of a slimy fish and apparently unable to even die, Jonah finally prays. Trapped inside a situation Jonah could never have conceived, he finally decided that it might be a good idea to talk to God.

Unfortunately, this has to happen to many of us as well. When we refuse to listen, to obey and turn to God, He sometimes allows a storm or a trial in our lives that places us in a situation where we feel helpless, hopeless, and trapped. First Jonah went down to Joppa. Then Jonah went down to the hold in the ship. Finally Jonah went way down into the heart of the sea, carried there by a great whale. Sometimes it takes getting this far down, this low, before we will realize that we need to look up.

In the belly of the whale, Jonah finally did just that. He *repented.* At the end of his prayer of repentance, Jonah promised obedience to God. He said, "I will sacrifice to You with the voice of thanksgiving. That which I have vowed I will pay. Salvation is from the LORD" (Jonah 2:9). After God saw that He had Jonah's will, He "commanded the fish, and it vomited Jonah up onto the dry land" (verse 10).

Last time we checked, Jonah was out in the middle of the sea. But all of a sudden he is vomited onto dry land. While Jonah is praying to God in the middle of his messed-up situation, the fish is taking Jonah somewhere. In fact, Jonah's judgment—being swallowed by a fish—is actually taking him to where God wants him to be. The fish isn't taking Jonah to Nineveh. The fish is taking Jonah right back to Joppa, back to the place of his disobedience. God takes Jonah to his place of departure to give him another chance to do the right thing.

Again, Jonah is faced with a decision. Is he going to buy another ticket to Tarshish, or is he going to go to Nineveh this time, as God had asked—and as God would ask once again. That's the good news about God. He will repeat Himself if necessary. Jonah missed God's call the first time, but he got another chance. This second chance is recorded for us in Jonah 3:1-2. We read, "Now the word of the LORD came to Jonah the second time, saying, 'Arise, go to Nineveh the great city and proclaim to it the proclamation which I am going to tell you.'"

Notice that this time God didn't give Jonah the rest of the information. He didn't trust Jonah with what he was going to proclaim until Jonah had made the decision to follow Him. God does that with us at times too. We want to know all of the details ahead of time so we can make our decision based on what we see and think, but God wants to teach us to walk by faith. He wants to see whether the prayer we prayed in the belly of our whale of a situation—"That which I have vowed I will pay"—is genuine. Or are we going to change our minds and revert back to our natural ways once God has rescued us from the abyss of life's trials?

Repentance in Ninevah

This time our prophet had learned his lesson. So Jonah obeyed. The passage tells us that without hesitation, "Jonah arose and went to Nineveh according to the word of the LORD" (verse 3). No boat rides. No naps. No being thrown into the sea. Rather, Jonah got up and headed straight to Nineveh.

Once he got there, Jonah walked for one full day through the city telling them that they would be destroyed in 40 days. Jonah's sermon wasn't very long. It wasn't even very deep. Jonah simply told them that they would be overthrown in 40 days. Jonah gave the Ninevites some pretty bad news. But the good news is that the 40 days meant there was time to reverse their situation. God could have destroyed them right then, but the warning came with a time element, and the citizens of Nineveh paid great attention.

God had not yet sent judgment, so the Ninevites had an opportunity to repent. Repentance gives God the freedom to withhold His discipline. Nineveh's wickedness had come up to God, as we saw in chapter 1. They had accumulated a boatload of wrath that God was about to unload on them. But in His mercy, He gave them 40 days to do something about it.

And they did. Nineveh was a large city. It would take an average person three days just to cover all of the ground in this enormous city. But after only one day of Jonah's preaching on the street corners and in the alleys, the city responded—even the king himself. As a result of Jonah's obedience to God, he became the only preacher in history to save an entire city through one sermon. The response was instant and authentic.

> Then the people of Nineveh believed in God; and they called a fast and put on sackcloth from the greatest to the least of them. When the word reached the king of Nineveh, he arose from his throne, laid aside his robe from him, covered himself with sackcloth and sat on the ashes. He issued a proclamation and it said, "In Nineveh by the decree of the king and his nobles: Do not let man, beast, herd, or flock taste a thing. Do not let them eat or drink water. But both man and beast must be covered with sackcloth; and let men call on God earnestly that each may turn from his wicked way and from the violence which is in his hands. Who knows, God may turn and relent and withdraw His burning anger so that we will not perish" (Jonah 3:5-9).

Jonah had just ushered in the greatest revival in human history involving one of the most wicked and violent groups of people who had ever lived. The people repented. The king repented. The nobles repented. Even the animals repented, or at least they attempted to. The king commanded everyone to get their dogs, cows, bulls, and goats down on their knees to repent because he wanted to make sure God knew this was a serious repentance. A simple gospel message, "Forty days and Nineveh will be destroyed," turned a whole city around. The fire-and-brimstone preaching evangelist had just witnessed the greatest evangelistic response in the history of mankind simply because he finally decided to do what God had originally told him to do.

Think about the power in this story. A rebel like Jonah running from the very presence of God ends up being the greatest evangelist of all time. Yet he almost missed it all because he couldn't see past his own wants or desires.

God wanted Jonah to walk by faith. For all Jonah knew, the Ninevites could have skinned him alive and hung him up for show-and-tell. Instead, they made him the preacher who would forever be recorded in history as having delivered the message that saved an entire city. God doesn't always explain what He's doing in advance. In fact, He rarely does. Often God wants us to take a faith step first so we can discover what He's up to. Jonah went to Nineveh, preached a simple sermon, and changed the course of an entire nation. You would think he might enjoy some satisfaction at that point. You would think he might feel tremendously blessed to have been rescued from a fish, used by God, and spared by the Ninevites.

But Jonah didn't see things that way. Jonah didn't recognize the accomplishment God performed through him. Jonah's focus was on the temporal and what he could see rather than on what God was doing in history for eternity. All Jonah knew was that he had just evangelized his enemies. God had shown them mercy. And he was angry.

> It greatly displeased Jonah and he became angry. He prayed to the LORD and said, "Please LORD, was not this what I said while I was still in my own country? Therefore in order to forestall this I fled to Tarshish, for I knew that You are a gracious and compassionate God, slow to anger and abundant in lovingkindness, and one who relents concerning calamity. Therefore now, O LORD, please take my life from me, for death is better to me than life" (Jonah 4:1-3).

This is the point in the story when Jonah loses it. He's been messed up before, but at this point he is talking nothing but crazy. Jonah has just seen an entire city get saved, and he's telling God he doesn't want any of them in heaven—he doesn't want any of them to receive mercy.

"Kill me instead, God," Jonah says. "Because if you are going to spare all of these people, then I don't want to live to see it." Jonah knows that if the Ninevites are saved, he's going to have to treat them like brothers and sisters. And he doesn't want to do that. He has gotten so used to viewing them and treating them like enemies that he doesn't want things to change.

Have you ever known someone that you didn't want to get right with God? You might not have hated that person, but maybe you thought that if they got right with God, you would have to treat them like a brother or a sister in Christ, and you didn't want to. That's how Jonah felt. But Jonah was also surprised. He knew that God was a compassionate God—He had said so and demonstrated it at other times—but Jonah was probably surprised that the Ninevites had it within themselves to respond. They were too evil. Yet this is a great example to each of us that there may be people in our lives who we think could never get saved, but perhaps they are on the verge of being saved and they just need to hear something from you.

You never know what God is doing on the inside while you and I are silent on the outside. Maybe you have a cousin, brother-in-law, neighbor, coworker, or friend who is on the verge of eternity, and God has asked you to open up your mouth to let them know about Him. Don't look at what you can see because God is often working behind the scenes to prepare people to respond to Him.

Jonah Questions God Again

God responded to Jonah's disgust with a question. God asked Jonah, "Do you have good reason to be angry?" (Jonah 4:4).

It wasn't a question in need of a response. God was pointing out that just because Jonah was angry didn't mean his anger was justified. He wanted Jonah to consider whether his anger was legitimate or illegitimate. But at this point, Jonah didn't seem to care whether his anger was legitimate. He had become so enraged at this point that he decided to go east of the city to make a shelter for himself in hopes that God would destroy the city anyhow.

Sitting underneath the shade he had made for himself, Jonah waited to see what God was going to do to the city. Surely God wouldn't forgive the entire city. After all, those people were evil. While Jonah waited underneath the hot sun, God made a plant grow up over him to give him more shade than he had made for himself. The text tells us that this made Jonah happy. So Jonah has now gone from angry to happy in the span of a few verses. But God decided to appoint a worm to eat the plant the next morning and remove the shade He had given to Jonah. Then God also appointed a scorching wind and the hot sun to beat down on Jonah. Sweltering in the heat, Jonah's happiness went back to despair as he said, "Death is better to me than life" (verse 8).

Jonah has gone from despair to anger to happiness to suicidal thoughts all in a matter of a day. Either Jonah was bipolar or God was definitely messing with him to make a point. I believe the latter is correct. God was messing with him in order to help Jonah to grow spiritually, just as God will sometimes bring situations into our lives in order to help us grow spiritually. When a person gets mad at the wrong stuff rather than the right stuff, he or she is being spiritually immature. Jonah was a prophet, but he was acting like a kid.

So God made an appointment to teach him another lesson.

We're seeing a lot of appointments in this story about Jonah. In chapter 1, God appoints a great fish to swallow Jonah. In chapter 4, God appoints a plant to grow up over Jonah. Later, God appoints a worm to attack the plant. After that, He appoints a scorching wind to beat down on Jonah.

These appointments serve as reminders that the things that are happening in your life might not just be the result of a bad day. Maybe they aren't just an irritating coworker or family member or a negative situation. Maybe God is appointing a certain thing or person in your life in order to grow you spiritually. Next time, rather than getting mad at the situation or person, ask God to show you what He's up to with this trial. Ask Him to reveal to you what it is He is trying to get you to see.

He does for Jonah. God explains it to Jonah after Jonah complains yet again that he wants to die because, this time, the plant is gone.

> You had compassion on the plant for which you did not work and which you did not cause to grow, which came up overnight and perished overnight. Should I not have compassion on Nineveh, the great city in which there are more than 120,000 persons who do not know the difference between their right and left hand, as well as many animals? (verses 10-11).

As long as God was taking care of Jonah, Jonah was happy. But as soon as God wanted to take care of someone else, Jonah was angry. He didn't have God's heart. In fact, many of us do not have God's heart. If we're happy only as long as God is doing something for us, if we never want to see Him doing something for somebody else, then we don't have His heart.

You cannot expect to be a recipient of God's grace and refuse to be a dispenser of it. If you're not willing to dispense it, you won't receive it. You can't say to God, "Be good to me, but don't ask me to be good to anyone else." It doesn't work that way. God wants to bless you, but first He needs to see whether He can bless others through you. The world doesn't need any more constipated Christians. I realize the illustration is crude, but I hope you get the point. A true blessing is given to you, but it's also intended to flow through you to minister to and bless someone else.

Jonah's story doesn't end with him sitting on the hillside, saddened that the people he preached repentance to actually responded. The conclusion of Jonah's story is found several books later in the Bible—in the New Testament.

Some of the scribes and Pharisees said to Him, "Teacher, we want to see a sign from You." But He answered and said to them, "An evil and adulterous generation craves for a sign; and yet no sign will be given to it but the sign of Jonah the prophet; for just as Jonah was three days and three nights in the belly of the sea monster, so will the Son of Man be three days and three nights in the heart of the earth. The men of Nineveh will stand up with this generation at the judgment, and will condemn it because they repented at the preaching of Jonah; and behold, something greater than Jonah is here" (Matthew 12:38-41).

This passage occurs immediately following Jesus' deliverance of a man possessed by demons. Jesus not only delivered the man but also opened his eyes so he could see and opened his mouth so he could talk. But the Pharisees weren't satisfied with miracles. They wanted more. So they asked Jesus to do something else to prove that He was who He said He was.

Jesus caught the Pharisees in their trick, though. They weren't really looking for a sign at all. They were just looking for another reason to point their finger at Him. However, He chose to give them the sign of Jonah. When Jonah came out of the belly of the fish after three days and three nights, one of the world's most evil nations immediately repented. Things changed drastically. Jesus let the Pharisees know that someone greater than Jonah was in their midst and that they needed to be on the lookout for what was about to occur.

This brings us to some good news for you and me. If a rebel preacher named Jonah could change an entire city by preaching the simple, straightforward word of God, how much more change can Jesus Christ bring about when His words are made manifest in our lives?

If Jonah, as broken and messed up as he was, could usher in

a turnaround unlike any other throughout all of history, then we should have no doubts whatsoever that Jesus Christ, as perfect and sinless as He is, can turn around any situation in our lives that needs to be restored.

"Something greater than Jonah is here," friend. And He has all of the power, grace, mercy, and wisdom you need to endure whatever it is you're facing, whether you are like Jonah in the storm, in the fish, sitting on the hill…or even if you are a Ninevite yourself. It's all available to redeem you wherever you are if you will simply let Him. God's compassion is new every morning. Great is His faithfulness. I encourage you to be like Moses, Rahab, Jacob, and even Jonah. Take God at His word and start living the destiny He has created you for today.

It's never too late for God to turn things around. Don't take the detour like Jonah.

Respond to God right from the start.

5

Esther Was a Diva

Esther was a diva. She is introduced as a young lady who was "beautiful of form and face" (Esther 2:7). The NIV says Esther "had a lovely figure and was beautiful."

The name Esther literally means "star." If Esther lived today, she would have her own reality show called the *The Esther Experience*, and people could tune in daily to view the diva in action. Her pictures would regularly be found on the covers of *W* magazine and *Vogue*. Tabloids would run stories about her: "Is Esther Too Thin?" "Does Esther Have a Baby Bump?" "What Is Esther Wearing, and Where Did She Buy It?"

Esther wasn't merely easy on the eyes. She wasn't just pretty. No, Esther was much more than that. The text makes it clear that Esther was beyond pretty. Esther was beautiful. Whatever the gene pool happened to be that brought Esther into being, it definitely worked in her favor because she was, as they say where I come from, *fine*. To really say it correctly, you have to drag the *i* out a bit. Esther was *fiiiiine*.

Yet even though Esther was fine in both form and face, her life started out as an uphill battle. Orphaned as a young girl, Esther—also known as Hadassah—was taken in by her relative Mordecai. Esther 2:7 tells us that Mordecai raised Esther as his own daughter. Both of them undoubtedly lived difficult lives as minorities and exiles in a foreign land.

Yet despite the harsh reality of Esther's existence, her story has been preserved for more than 2500 years as a tale of beauty, bravery, and even a bit of divalike behavior. When Esther was challenged to risk her own life to potentially save the lives of others, she initially balked. She played the diva card and stalled. That's when Mordecai challenged her to think beyond herself by saying a line that may be better known than Bogart's, "Here's looking at you, kid." Mordecai said, "And who knows whether you have not attained royalty for such a time as this?" (Esther 4:14).

For such a time as this.

It's a phrase quoted in churches and small groups and printed in Christian newsletters, magazines, and books. It's a phrase that encapsulates the power of personal destiny, appealing to the hope in all of us. This is because deep within each of us is a desire to experience purpose and meaning beyond our own understanding and our own abilities and decisions. We were created for *this*. We want our own renditions of the Esther experience. Maybe that's why Esther's story appeals to such a broad audience. In Esther's story, we come face-to-face with the potential of our own life story and God's providence.

The Power of Providence

Providence is the hand of God in the glove of history. Nowhere in the Bible are God's invisible fingerprints shown more clearly than in the book of Esther. In fact, Esther is the only book in the Bible where God's fingerprints are the only evidence of His presence. It doesn't even include His name. If you start reading from the very first verse of Esther all the way through to the closing chapter, you will not come across God's name even once. That cannot be said of any other book in the Bible.

Not only is God's name not found, but neither are there any references to God's people sacrificing to Him, worshipping Him, or serving Him. There are no references to the Word of God or even to His laws. This absence caused a stir when the books of the Old Testament were being compiled. After all, how could God author a book that didn't mention Him by name?

Yet while the name of God is not present in the book of Esther, His fingerprints are everywhere. The theological term for this is *providence*. Providence is the work of God whereby He integrates and blends events in order to fulfill His original design. Providence is God sitting behind the steering wheel of life. It refers to God's governance of all events as He directs them toward His intended end. Providence is God using what is frequently called luck, chance, coincidence, or mistakes to stitch events together into a tapestry of meaning.

God's providential dealings often happen behind the scenes. Like the great and powerful Oz behind the curtain, God isn't always directly seen in what He does. Unlike the great Oz behind the curtain, God isn't a fake, and He *is* always directly involved in what is happening.

Yet sometimes we label as a mistake what God has done on purpose. Things might look completely out of order in the visible realm when they are perfectly in order in the spiritual realm, having been arranged in a way that brings about God's perfect plan.

Each Wednesday night at our church, I set aside a time to answer questions about the Bible from the congregation. It's more informal than when I deliver a sermon. In this setting I hear what's on the hearts of church members and address practical issues of living out the Christian life.

Not too long ago, one of the questions was why God's name was absent from the book of Esther. No one knows the answer for sure, but we do know that when the story of Esther took place, God's people were living outside of God's will. God had instructed them to go back to Israel from Babylon, but many of them did not go back, choosing instead to stay where they had become comfortable. Living as the minority culture in a foreign land must have been challenging. But regardless, the people of Israel had become accustomed to their way of life, their community, and their day-to-day activities. They had become at home outside the will of God. In fact, they had become so at home there that Mordecai himself willingly placed Esther in a position of moral compromise—a situation where she would be required to sleep with the king without being married to him.

People can start to feel at home outside the will of God. Just as Jonah fell asleep in the middle of a thundering storm that God had sent to shake him up, a person can get so comfortable being out of the will of God that it seems like too much trouble to get back in it.

Because the book of Esther takes place in a context of a people living outside of God's will, as well as for other reasons, God takes a step back, not even allowing His name to be used in it. Yet even without the direct mention of God's name, this book contains some of the greatest and most profound spiritual principles. If you will truly grasp and own the principles found in the book of Esther, they can literally change the course of your life. If an unknown and foreign orphan girl named Esther can become the queen of a kingdom, there is nothing that God cannot do.

God's Cosmic Blender

You probably have a blender in your kitchen. Blenders have been uniquely designed to take independent foods and integrate, unite, interface, mix, and join them together to create something new and better than any of the items could have been on its own.

Just to keep the record straight, I don't cook. In fact, boiling water one time almost got me into trouble because I forgot to turn off the burner and then proceeded to take a nap. Yet even though I can't claim to be much of a cook, I do know that a blender puts different ingredients together so that they are amalgamated into something brand-new. Throw some ice cubes, strawberries, orange juice, and a banana together in a blender, and the end result is a fruit smoothie that is much tastier than any of the individual items.

What a blender does in your kitchen, God does in His universe. God is the consummate blender. He has an astounding ability to take seemingly unrelated things and put them together to form something bigger, better, and more beautiful than what each one was on its own. And no story in the Bible better illustrates God's ability to do this than the story of Esther. In Esther, we witness God perfectly intersecting plot lines and people in order to bring about His intended purpose.

Vashti Is Vanquished

We are first introduced to the story of Esther when the Persian king Ahasuerus, ruler of provinces from India to Ethiopia, decided to have a banquet. In fact, Ahasuerus didn't just have one banquet. This party king had at least five banquets, all recorded in the first two chapters of Esther.

At Ahasuerus' banquets, the men were in one location and the women were in another. One night while drunk, Ahasuerus sent seven eunuchs to bring his queen, Vashti, to his side of the party. Ahasuerus wanted to display Vashti's beauty before all of the men at the party. Now when a person becomes drunk, he quits thinking rationally and sometimes does unexpected things, such as summoning his wife to show her off before all of the other drunk men at the party. More than likely, that meant much more than just having Vashti strut the runway once or twice. It probably meant some form of uncovering or disclosure that Vashti apparently didn't feel comfortable with.

We know that Vashti didn't want to come at Ahasuerus' command because in Esther 1:12 we read that she refused. "Nope, not doing that," Vashti said (in my Tony Evans' paraphrase). "You're a fool, A-has, if you think I'm going to come and put myself out there in front of your whistle-blowing friends. It's not happening."

Vashti's refusal upset Ahasuerus so much that "his wrath burned within him" (verse 12). He asked the princes what should be done about a queen who refused to come when he called. This question got a well-thought-out reply by one of the princes named Memucan.

> Queen Vashti has wronged not only the king but also all the princes and all the peoples who are in all the provinces of King Ahasuerus. For the queen's conduct will become known to all the women causing them to look with contempt on their husbands by saying, "King Ahasuerus commanded Queen Vashti to be brought in to his presence, but she did not come." This day the ladies of Persia and Media who have heard of the queen's conduct will speak in the same way to all the king's princes, and there will be plenty of contempt and anger. If it pleases the king, let a royal edict be issued by him and let it be written in the laws of Persia and Media so that it cannot be repealed, that Vashti may no longer come into the presence of King Ahasuerus, and let the king give her royal position to another who is more worthy than she (Esther 1:16-19).

Basically, Memucan said that word was going to spread through the kingdom that the king's wife resisted him and his request, and when that happens, everyone is going to have problems with their wives as well. Women will start marching or protesting because if Vashti doesn't have to respond to her husband's requests, neither should they. If the king can't run his own house, the princes warned, it's going to create a terrible situation for every other man in all 127 provinces that he ruled.

After hearing the prince's council, Ahasuerus quickly got rid of Vashti. He put her out of his kingdom, banning her from her role and his presence for the rest of her life. However, not long after that, the party was over. And when it was, our king sobered up. Once he got sober and his anger decreased, Ahasuerus thought about what he had done. We read, "After these things when the anger of King Ahasuerus had subsided, he remembered Vashti and what she had done and what had been decreed against her" (Esther 2:1).

In other words, he came to his senses. He had temporarily lost his mind and made a law that he now regretted. The problem, though, was that the law of the Medes and the Persians simply stated that when the king made a decree, no one—not even the king himself—could reverse it.

In a span of just a few days, Ahasuerus has gone from partying and drinking to being lonely and depressed. He has banished his beautiful wife, Vashti, and now he misses her. So the king's attendants came up with another idea.

> Let beautiful young virgins be sought for the king. Let the king appoint overseers in all the provinces of his kingdom that they may gather every beautiful young virgin to the citadel of Susa, to the harem, into the custody of Hegai, the king's eunuch, who is in charge of the women; and let their cosmetics be given them. Then let the young lady who pleases the king be queen in place of Vashti (Esther 2:2-4).

Rather than have him mope around all day long about a regrettable decision, the attendants suggested that the king simply start his own *Next Top Queen* search. Surely there were other women like Vashti who could be his wife. And to make matters easier, they even offered to go on the road and conduct preliminary screenings in every province of his kingdom. He wouldn't have to do a thing. The best of the best would get a yellow ticket to Susa in their quest to be crowned Ahasuerus' next queen.

Ahasuerus seemed to like the idea of starring in a season of *The Bachelor-King*, and he gave the command to his attendants to begin the search for the lucky woman who would be the last one standing as he handed her his red rose.

Episode 1 began with Esther making a great first impression on those who could help or hurt her fate.

> So it came about when the command and decree of the king were heard and many young ladies were gathered to the citadel of Susa into the custody of Hegai, that Esther was taken to the king's palace into the custody of Hegai, who was in charge of the women. Now the young lady pleased him and found favor with him. So he quickly provided her with her cosmetics and food, gave her seven choice maids from the king's palace and transferred her and her maids to the best place in the harem. Esther did not make known her people or her kindred, for Morde- cai had instructed her that she should not make them known (verses 8-10).

We see through this passage that Mordecai had made it clear to Esther that all she needed to do was show up and look beautiful, but that she wasn't to tell anyone that she was an Israelite. To do so in Susa would not have worked well for her. So Esther followed Mordecai's advice, and in so doing, she found favor with Hegai, who not only provided her with the best location, cosmetics, and food, but also would later give Esther advice in her quest to land the king of Persia.

In episode 2, we find Esther and all of the other bride hopefuls spending the next 12 months preparing themselves in the harem with every possible form of beauty treatments available in that day.

Now when the turn of each young lady came to go in to the King Ahasuerus, after the end of her twelve months under the regulations for the women—for the days of their beautification were completed as follows: six months with oil of myrrh and six months of spices and the cosmetics for women...(verse 12).

Each woman spent six months in each beauty regimen, but as we have already seen, Esther had found favor with Hegai, the eunuch in charge of the women. So Esther received not only the best beauty treatments but also the best food during that time. After the 12 months of preparation had concluded, we reach episode 3, when it's time for Esther to make her presence known to the king.

The young lady would go in to the king in this way: anything that she desired was given to her to take with her from the harem to the king's palace. In the evening she would go in and in the morning she would return to the second harem, to the custody of Shaashgaz, the king's eunuch who was in charge of the concubines. She would not again go in to the king unless the king delighted in her and she was summoned by name.

Now when the turn of Esther, the daughter of Abihail the uncle of Mordecai who had taken her as his daughter, came to go in to the king, she did not request anything except what Hegai, the king's eunuch who was in charge of the women, advised. And Esther found favor in the eyes of all who saw her. So Esther was taken to King Ahasuerus to his royal palace in the tenth month which is the month Tebeth, in the seventh year of his reign (Esther 2:13-16).

When it came time for Esther to visit the king in his palace, she chose to take only that which Hegai, the king's eunuch, had advised her to take. Hegai knew what would please the king, and because Hegai favored Esther, he sent her to the king with everything that would help to make the best impression on him. And his plan worked.

Episode 4 gives us the king's decision. "The king loved Esther more than all the women, and she found favor and kindness with him more than all the virgins, so that he set the royal crown on her head and made her queen instead of Vashti" (verse 17). Esther had won both the title and the crown as queen next to King Ahasuerus. But remember, we are only in episode 4. There is a lot more of this season that still needs to play out.

Introducing Haman

The season heats up as we're introduced to another character in the story named Haman. In chapter 3 of Esther, we learn that Haman has been promoted to a high position by King Ahasuerus. In fact, Haman's position is so high that his mere presence demands a response from the king's servants. However, as we will read in verse 2, Mordecai—Esther's relative—refuses to bow before him: "All the king's servants who were at the king's gate bowed down and paid homage to Haman; for so the king had commanded concerning him. But Mordecai neither bowed down nor paid homage."

Mordecai's refusal to pay homage to Haman, along with the fact that he was a foreigner, enraged Haman. In fact, Haman was so full of rage, he wasn't content to make Mordecai alone suffer for his decision. Haman decided to make all of Mordecai's people, the Jews, suffer as well. In fact, Haman comes up with a plan to annihilate the Jews.

So now we have a Persian king who has deposed his queen because she wouldn't respond to him the way he had wanted. We've met a beautiful girl—Esther, the Jewish orphan—who has caught the king's eye and become the queen of the kingdom. We also have the evil

Haman, who has been promoted to a position that requires others to bow down to him. We also have another man—Mordecai, a cousin of the queen—who refuses to bow to Haman. Now Haman wants to kill an entire race of people, the same race as the beautiful queen, because his pride has been tampered with by a man of that race. And we are only partway through the story. The book of Esther relates a story of intrigue, suspense, loyalty, pride, love, defiance, and beauty thus far. Basically, it's a soap opera tucked away between Nehemiah and Job.

Fast-forwarding through a few more episodes, we come to the end of chapter 3 and the king's irreversible decree to annihilate the Jews. When Mordecai hears of the impending doom brought onto his people all because he wouldn't bow to Haman, he tears his clothes, puts on sackcloth and ashes, and goes to the middle of the city to wail loudly in public. Feeling personally responsible, Mordecai sends a message to Esther giving her a copy of the text of the edict that declares the upcoming destruction of the Jews, hoping she will go to the king and plead with him to do something.

Mordecai had told Esther not to reveal that she is a Jew. But now she's living in the palace with the king and the Jews are slated for genocide, so Mordecai tells her that now is the time to reveal her true identity. The king chose her for a reason. Surely he will listen to her plea.

Esther, heartbroken for her cousin and her people, sends a message back to Mordecai explaining why she's helpless to do anything to stop the decree. Decrees cannot be revoked, and everyone knows whoever enters the king's presence without having been invited risks being killed. Basically, Esther plays the diva card and lets Mordecai know that he doesn't understand how things work in the palace. A person in Esther's position doesn't simply march into the presence of the king and tell him what she's thinking. In fact, Esther goes so far as to tell Mordecai that she and the king haven't even hooked up recently. It's been a month, and the king hasn't even asked for her.

> All the king's servants and the people of the king's provinces know that for any man or woman who comes to the king to the inner court who is not summoned, he has but one law, that he be put to death, unless the king holds out to him the golden scepter so that he may live. And I have not been summoned to come to the king for these thirty days (Esther 4:11).

Esther knows she's come from rags to riches—from the outhouse to the white house. She used to wash her own clothes by hand, and now she has maids to wash them for her. She used to fetch her own water in a jug, but now she bathes daily in warm baths drawn for her. She's traded in her walking shoes for a Mercedes chariot and exchanged Target for Neiman Marcus. Those things aren't bad, but Esther has begun to believe her own reviews. She has bought into the meaning of her own name—that she is a star. And to help out someone else by appearing uninvited before the king is just too risky for a star. After all, Esther could lose more than everything she has; she could lose her life. So, in a manner of words, Esther tells Mordecai, "Nope, not happening."

Mordecai gets the note from Esther and sends another note straight back to her. This is the child he had rescued from an impossible situation. This is the cousin he called his own daughter. Mordecai wasn't about to take a *nope* as Esther's final answer.

> Do not imagine that you in the king's palace can escape any more than all the Jews. For if you remain silent at this time, relief and deliverance will arise for the Jews from another place and you and your father's house will perish. And who knows whether you have attained royalty *for such a time as this*? (verses 13-14).

Mordecai reminds Hadassah, now known solely as Esther, that even though she's living a luxurious life in the palace, she won't escape Haman's wrath any more than the next Jew in the kingdom. A king's edict is a final edict. More than that, Mordecai reminds Esther that although she might be in a unique position to help her people, if she doesn't step up to deliver them, God will find someone else who can do the same job. Mordecai reminds Esther that she is not indispensable. If she won't cooperate with God, He can find someone who will. Ahasuerus already got rid of one wife, Vashti, in the span of one party. Getting rid of the second one might not be that difficult.

Mordecai was trying to help Esther make the connection between her beauty, her opportunity, and the kingdom of God. She had not yet understood that how she looked and the position she held were tied to a kingdom purpose. All she thought was that she was fortunate because she could dress up and look fine, grabbing the eye of the king. But God had specifically placed Esther in a position of influence, combining her background, history, and personality in such a way as to deliver His people. It wasn't just about her fine clothes, furniture, lifestyle, hairstyle, and bank account. The favor Esther had received was about much more than all of that.

For Such a Time as This

I realize this story is from a time long ago in a kingdom far away, but the principles are as relevant as if it happened today. Have you ever considered that maybe God has you here in His kingdom on earth *for such a time as this*? Have you ever considered that everything that has happened in your life—the good, bad, and the ugly—has happened for a specific purpose up to this point? If all you see is what you see, you haven't seen the kingdom yet.

God's kingdom involves His rule, His purposes, and His agenda. In the kingdom, one overarching principle rings true: You are blessed in order to be a blessing. You are freed in order to set free. You are redeemed in order to redeem.

. Maybe you've been blessed with an excellent education, or great looks, or even a good life. Whatever God has given you—be it a talent, gift, or unique capacity in life—He has done it on purpose. He doesn't want you to hoard your blessings, but to use the position He has given you to bring about His purposes in the lives of others around you.

Esther feared going before the king because she thought that doing so would mean trouble. If he didn't hold out his scepter, she could lose her life. But Esther's fears were rooted in one thing: Esther. When the greatest thing that matters to you is you, then even if you are in the kingdom, you will miss the point of the kingdom altogether. Just as Esther almost did, you will miss out on the kingdom-sized destiny God has just for you.

After Mordecai's reply, Esther finally got it. She connected who she was and the position she was in with God's purposes. When she did so, she sent back a much different reply to Mordecai.

> Go, assemble all the Jews who are found in Susa, and fast for me; do not eat or drink for three days, night or day. I and my maidens also will fast in the same way. And thus I will go in to the king, which is not according to the law; and if I perish, I perish (verse 16).

People often take a risk in life for a business deal, or a thrill, or even a relationship. Why not take a risk for God? Esther did. She decided to take the risk—with the appropriate planning and preparation.

Esther's plan involved asking all the Jews in Susa to fast and pray for her for three days and nights. She and her maidens would also pray and fast. After this, she would go to the king and risk her life to save her people.

As Esther was making plans to visit the king, she didn't know that God was working His cosmic blender in the background once again. All Esther could see was that in a few days she had to approach a man who had shown no interest in her for the past 30 days. Not only that, she had to approach a man who had banished his previous wife just because he was drunk one night and she didn't do what he had requested. This is the same man who could have Esther killed simply by not extending his golden scepter, the same man who had given in to Haman's wishes to annihilate an entire people group simply because Haman wanted him to.

Even so, after three days Esther approached the king. I'm sure you could have heard a pin drop in the room as Esther made her appearance before him without having been summoned. Seconds probably seemed like minutes or even hours as the two met eyes and Esther waited on the king's response.

> When the king saw Esther the queen standing in the court, she obtained favor in his sight; and the king extended to Esther the golden scepter which was in his hand. So Esther came near and touched the top of the scepter (Esther 5:2).

She had survived. The first part of the challenge was over, and Esther had received favor from the king. But the story couldn't end there. Esther still needed to speak on behalf of her people. At this point, Esther planned to invite the king and Haman to dinner so she could do just that. But what Esther didn't know is that while she was preparing herself for that next step—the dinner—God was working behind the scenes. Haman had decided to build a gallows to hang Mordecai and his family on as a prelude to the killing of the Jews. At the same time, the king had a rough night, and everything in Esther's story thus far hinges on this one night.

> During the night the king could not sleep so he gave an order to bring the book of records, the chronicles, and they were read before the king. It was found written

what Mordecai had reported concerning Bigthana and Teresh, two of the king's eunuchs who were doorkeepers, that they had sought to lay hands on King Ahasuerus. The king said, "What honor or dignity has been bestowed on Mordecai for this?" Then the king's servants who attended him said, "Nothing has been done for him" (Esther 6:1-3).

The king couldn't sleep. That may seem like a minor thing. After all, I'm sure the king had many sleepless nights. But what matters is that the king couldn't sleep *this* night. On this night, the king requests someone to come and read to him in order to put him to sleep and stop his tossing and turning. He calls for the record keeper. You can't get much more boring than that. There is nothing like reading the minutes of a board meeting to put you fast asleep.

But as the records are being read, the king notices something—someone had saved his life. That seems pretty important, the king thinks. He asks his servant what had been done for the person who saved his life. "Nothing," the servant replies. The king doesn't like that at all, so the next day he calls Haman in and asks him what should be done for someone he wants to honor. Haman, thinking the king must be planning to honor him, gives him a great reply.

> Let them bring a royal robe which the king has worn, and the horse on which the king has ridden, and on whose head a royal crown has been placed; and let the robe and the horse be handed over to one of the king's most noble princes and let them array the man whom the king desires to honor and lead him on horseback through the city square, and proclaim before him, "Thus it shall be done to the man whom the king desires to honor" (verses 8-9).

Great idea, the king agrees. In fact, since Haman has all of the details down so clearly, Ahasuerus decides to let Haman carry out the plan himself—with one slight change from what Haman had envisioned. This honor belongs to Mordecai. Mordecai, the man Haman was about to hang, is now the man the king has ordered him to honor. The tables were turned overnight simply because the king could not go to sleep.

That is how great God is. God works behind the scenes—keeping people awake when they ought to be sleeping—when people step out as Esther did and take a risk to be used by Him.

Esther didn't witness God moving behind the scenes until she went forward and took the risk. Once she did that, God went to work setting the stage for the next episode. Proverbs 21:1 tells us, "The king's heart is like channels of water in the hand of the LORD; He turns it wherever He wishes." That's good news for you and me. The king is the most powerful man in the world, and if his heart is in God's hand, then whose hand is your boss' heart in? Whose hand is your family member's heart in? Whose hand is your present circumstance in? If God can direct an entire government and save a nation simply by keeping the king awake, He can certainly fix whatever mess you might be in if you will step out in faith.

When I was younger, I caught a glimpse of God working behind the scenes on my behalf. While in seminary, I worked the night shift at the Trailways bus station. It was called the dead-man shift because it lasted all night long. After a few weeks on the job, I was approached about a scheme the employees had going on. Someone would punch you in even though you weren't in, and you could sleep an hour longer than your normal break allowed. Essentially, you would get paid for sleeping.

When they came to me and told me how the system worked, I told them that I couldn't take part in their scheme. As a Christian, I couldn't do that. Their response was simple: "You don't have a choice. Everyone does it."

Again I replied, "I'm sorry, but as a follower of Jesus Christ, I can't participate in your scam." Needless to say, the rest of the employees didn't like that and tried to punish me for not participating. For example, when five of us were supposed to be unloading a bus, the other four would sit down and watch me do it by myself. Scenarios like that played out for an entire month simply because I wouldn't go along with their deception.

But while this was going on, God was working things out behind the scenes. One evening I got a call to come to the front office. The person I met with in the front office told me that they had a suspicion about what was going on during the night shift and that they had sent one of the supervisors to go around at night and check it out. The supervisor noticed that most everyone was taking part in the scam but that I wasn't. As a result, they promoted me over everyone else and made me the night supervisor.

While I was unloading buses all by myself and the others were sleeping, God was working behind the scenes. God can work it out, friend. Trust me. I've seen it in my own life—not just at Trailways, but in many scenarios. God can work things out while people are sleeping, just as my fellow employees were at the bus station. Or, as in the case of King Ahasuerus, He can work things out while someone can't go to sleep at all. We might call it luck, chance, or coincidence, but providence is the invisible hand of God orchestrating things for good. Just as God arranged for Ruth, a Moabite widow, to connect with Boaz, who would eventually marry her, and just as God arranged for Moses' mother to be hired to raise him, God is continually in the business of hooking people up to carry out His divine plan.

Haman Is Hanged

Or, as in the case of Haman, God can bring things together for bad. We read that when Haman got the news of what he was going to have to do for Mordecai, the man he was just days away from hanging on his gallows, he "hurried home, mourning, with his head covered" (Esther 6:12). Yet before Haman had much opportunity to cry at all, he was rushed to the banquet Esther had prepared for him and the king. At the banquet, king Ahasuerus asked Esther what it was that she wanted. "It shall be granted you…even to half of the kingdom it shall be done" (Esther 7:2).

But Esther told the king that she didn't want half of the kingdom. What she wanted was for her life and the lives of her people to be spared from an attack that had been planned against them. Enraged, the king asked Esther, "Who is he, and where is he, who would presume to do thus?" (verse 5). Esther pointed to Haman.

Haman was sobbing a few hours earlier, but now he's terrified before the king and queen. King Ahasuerus went outside into the palace garden to try to cool off from his anger, but Haman stayed behind in the room and begged Esther for his life. Apparently, Haman's pleading got out of hand.

> When the king returned from the palace garden into the place where they were drinking wine, Haman was falling on the couch where Esther was. Then the king said, "Will he even assault the queen with me in the house?" As the word went out of the king's mouth, they covered Haman's face (verse 8).

Immediately taking Haman out of the presence of the king and queen, "they hanged Haman on the gallows which he had prepared for Mordecai, and the king's anger subsided" (verse 10).

Friends, God is able to turn any situation around. The Bible is full of examples of God taking what looked like a hopeless situation—a too-late situation, a missed-shot opportunity—and turning it around. Consider Joseph, for example. He was sold into slavery, framed, and imprisoned in Egypt, but God worked it out so that he became next in line to the Pharaoh.

God turned things around for Joseph in Egypt and for Esther in

Susa, and He does it in our own lives too. God directs our paths to get us exactly where we are supposed to be.

According to my plan, I was never supposed to come to Dallas, where I eventually became the first African-American to graduate from Dallas Theological Seminary with a doctoral degree.

According to my plan, I was never supposed to stay in Dallas, where I have served as senior pastor of Oak Cliff Bible Fellowship for more than 35 years. And God saw fit to open doors in the early 1980s for me to spread His Word through a radio ministry when most major Christian radio stations resisted airing Black preachers to their listeners.

According to my plan, I was supposed to be studying in Indiana. But one of my college professors saw something in me and offered to pay for me to apply to a school that I thought was not even an option for me. I didn't even have the money to pay my application fee. But God spoke to a professor on my behalf, and because He did, my life has gone in a direction that I had never imagined.

Regardless of how impossible things may seem, I want to encourage you to never give up or quit on God. God can work out, in, through, and around any situation for your good and His greater glory. But what He won't do is acquiesce to your divahood. God won't bow to your Esther-dom. Remember, the name Esther means "star." And God is not impressed by anyone's stardom. After all, He is the One who gave what was needed in order to get there.

God is not impressed when He takes us from the bottom to the top and yet we are silent about His kingdom. When God receives no benefit from blessing us, we have failed to connect our blessings with God's purposes. God gave Esther favor wherever she went—not just so she would have favor, but so through her, God could empower His people to defend themselves from the impending attack. God never blesses you just for you. The fastest way to cut off your blessing is to keep your blessing just for you.

Never be a blessing diva, assuming that your blessing is only about you. If God sees that He cannot use you for His kingdom purposes, He will find someone else through whom His delivering power can come. This is the warning Mordecai gave to Esther early on.

We live in a pompous world, a world of celebrity. We think that if we have a nice home, or a nice car, or a nice job, or a nice bank account, or any number of things, we're above taking steps of faith, risky moves that God calls us to on behalf of others.

In our celebrity-style Christianity, we often elevate our royalty above our service. Yes, it's true that as a child of the King, you are a prince or a princess. You are royalty. But Jesus said He is looking for servants, not celebrities. He says, "The greatest among you shall be your servant" (Matthew 23:11). A truly great person recognizes the unique opportunity he or she has been given and hasn't forgotten where that opportunity came from and why it exists.

Make sure you never find yourself too blessed to be a blessing— or too blessed to be used. God wants to bless you, but He doesn't want you to play the diva card when He does bless you. He wants to make sure that when the time comes, you will be willing to be used by Him to help others in His name for His glory and His kingdom purposes.

We are all valuable to God. But some of us are more useful to Him, which in turn, increases the value we have already been given.

For example, if you and I were to walk together on a sandy beach, we would be walking on sand that is free. However, if we wanted to buy some of that sand to use it at a school playground, we would pay roughly $25 a bag for that free sand. If we needed that sand as sandpaper for a restoration project we were working on, we would be paying several dollars just for a few sheets. And in Silicon Valley, where companies use sand in the process of making computer chips, the free sand we had been walking on has now increased exponentially in value when connected with high-priced computer chips. It's a simple law of economics—value goes up as usefulness goes up. God's blessings in your life ought to make you more than just blessed; they ought to make you useful to His kingdom.

There's no doubt that Esther had been blessed. She had been placed in a unique position close to the king and was experiencing all the benefits of his favor. However, until Esther was willing to use her lifestyle to meet the need of her people because of her love for God and faith in Him, Esther's blessings would have remained just that—blessings and not a destiny. More than that, when it came time for the decree to be carried out against the Jews, Esther would have lost the blessings she had been given, including her life.

Friend, if you have been a diva—or the male version, a divo—remember who has made you and given you the talents, skills, looks, finances, or opportunities that you have. God is not interested in acquiescing to celebrities. Rather, He is interested in blessing servants whose hearts are committed to Him and committed to using what He has given them to help deliver others.

Mordecai told Esther that she had come to her position "for such a time as this." And so have you.

Wherever you are, get rid of the diva card. Don't play it. Instead, use what God has given you to help others while glorifying Him. God used a diva to save an entire group of people when she set herself aside and said, "If I perish, I perish."

6

Peter Was an Apostate

Peter was an apostate. Most of us don't use that word very much, which is probably a good thing. An apostate is one who denies the faith. Peter ducked out on Jesus, denying Him and everything He stood for when some folks started to mess with him. At the very moment when Peter publicly denied Christ, everything imploded. Like an age-old building collapsing when dynamite is lit all around it and in it, things instantly collapsed for Peter. To deny the faith as a believer is a hypocritical sin. And to do it not long after boasting that you would die for the faith is an even graver sin.

Peter had always played the role of Mr. Tough Man on the disciple squad. He could talk a good game, frequently framing his words in an attempt to elevate himself above the others. He was committed, dedicated, and loyal. Or so he said.

Our story begins when Jesus was preparing His disciples for His death. He had been talking to them about the day when He would no longer be with them. Things were going to be different, and He wanted them to understand that the One who had sent them out to sea and provided the largest catch they had ever made was soon going to be gone. The One who had fed thousands in the wilderness with just a little boy's lunch was soon going to be gone. The One who had cast out the demons and healed the sick wasn't going to be around anymore. So He wanted to make sure the disciples had learned what He had taught them—that authentic love is expressed through service and not merely through words.

Jesus knew that times were going to be tough and that the disciples were going to need one another. He also knew that when difficulties arise, the temptation is to bail. Yet if some of the disciples did bail out of a rough situation, they would leave the others high and dry. So on the night before His crucifixion, Jesus told the disciples of the upcoming struggle and warned them that they would all scatter because of it.

However, Peter vehemently denied that he would ever do anything like that. Peter, never at a lack for words, undoubtedly said a number of things. Both Luke and Matthew recorded Peter's response. In Luke 22:33 (NIV) we read, "Lord, I am ready to go with you to prison and to death." And in Matthew 26:33 (NIV) we read, "Even if all fall away on account of you, I never will." My Tony Evans paraphrase reads, "It ain't gonna happen, Jesus. I've got Your back. You can count on homeboy to keep You covered. I've got it."

However you choose to interpret Peter's response to Christ that night, one thing is certain—he was adamant that he was hooked up with Jesus through thick and thin. Yet actions done in public speak louder than words offered in private, and Peter's actions would soon prove him to be a liar.

In Luke 22:31-32 (NIV) we hear Jesus saying, "Simon, Simon, Satan has asked to sift all of you as wheat. But I have prayed for you, Simon, that your faith may not fail. And when you have turned back, strengthen your brothers." Jesus told Simon that Satan had asked permission to sift all of the disciples like wheat. But Jesus narrowed in on Simon. He specifically said that He was praying for Simon—that his faith may not fail—because He had a purpose for

Simon after the chaos had cleared. He wanted Simon to go on and strengthen his brothers, who would have scattered from fear.

A principle I don't want to gloss over too quickly is that Satan had to ask permission to bother with Christ's disciple before he could do it. To sift wheat meant to remove the sleeve off the grain in order to separate the two. Essentially, it ruined what was in existence, making it impossible to repair the wheat to how it originally was. Where I come from, we wouldn't say "sift you like wheat." We would say that Satan had asked permission to "jack you up." Yet we learn the comforting truth that Satan can't sift you like wheat or jack you up without permission. If you're God's child, Satan has to get permission first. Even the devil is underneath God's sovereign hand. He can't just go and do whatever he wants to do. Nothing can reach you without passing through God's hand.

But I struggle with something else, and you may struggle with it as well: Why did God allow Satan to mess with Peter and the disciples in the first place? Why does He allow Satan to mess with any of us for that matter? That's a question that will frustrate you quickly if you don't live with an eternal perspective. But just as painful workouts can take an athlete to a greater level of strength, trials and troubles can strengthen us if we allow them. God's goal for each of us is to become a mature Christian. God's method to bring us to maturity often includes trials.

When God allows trouble in our lives, He has a purpose. The struggles we face aren't the random chaotic messes they may appear to be. God always has a purpose for what He allows. Unfortunately, we often miss that purpose because we get too focused on our pain. However, we can dignify our difficulties by discovering the destiny God is taking us to through the trial.

A Lesson on Humility

Peter needed to learn a few lessons through a trial, as we will see. A thorough reading of Scripture shows us that Peter frequently thought he was "all that" and then some. But Jesus was trying to tell Peter through his trial that he wasn't quite who he thought he was. Peter's pride opened the door for Satan to ask God's permission to jack him up.

God sometimes allows the devil to influence us for one of two reasons. First, He will allow a trial to manifest a sin that we're unaware of or have minimized so greatly in our minds that we don't realize the seriousness of it. Second, God will grant Satan permission to target us in order to stimulate our spiritual development and growth. The apostle Paul offers one of the greatest explanations for the purposes of trials in our lives.

> And not only this, but we also exult in our tribulations, knowing that tribulation brings about perseverance; and perseverance, proven character; and proven character, hope; and hope does not disappoint, because the love of God has been poured out within our hearts through the Holy Spirit who was given to us (Romans 5:3-5).

Just as a butterfly develops the muscular strength to fly by struggling to exit the cocoon, we develop spiritual maturity and growth by persevering in trials. That is where our spiritual muscles become strong enough to live the life of faith that God has called each one of us to as a believer in Jesus Christ.

Jesus Prayed for Peter

Even so, it's easy to lose focus on God in the middle of a trial, just as it's easy to lose focus on the goal of a stronger body in the middle of a workout. Jesus knew it would be easy for Peter to give up and deny Him once Satan started in on him. That's why He told Peter that He was praying for him. "I have prayed for you, Simon," Jesus said, "that your faith may not fail."

Jesus prayed that despite what Peter was about to go through, and despite his failures and shortcomings, his faith would not fail. Peter was on the verge of walking into the darkest 24 hours of his life, and Jesus had just warned him about what was about to take place. While Peter was going through it, and even after it was over, Jesus wanted him to remember that He had prayed for him.

Jesus Christ was interceding on behalf of Peter, which brings us to an interesting question. If Jesus felt it was necessary to intercede for Peter, why didn't He just go ahead and stop Satan from sifting Peter like wheat altogether? Jesus and the Father could have denied Satan permission to sift Peter and the disciples. But He didn't. Perhaps Jesus knew that Peter would find a greater purpose in his pain—if he did not lose his faith.

Although Jesus was straightforward with Peter about what was going to happen to him and the other disciples, Peter didn't seem to pay much attention to what He had said. At least it seems like that to me. If Jesus Himself just told me that before the rooster belted its next song, I was going to deny Him, I think I would have checked myself into a Holiday Inn and locked the door, stuck the do-not-disturb sign on the handle, taken the phone off of the hook, turned off my iPad and cell phone, unplugged the television, and gone to bed. I think I would have tried my best to sleep right through those 24 hours so that the terrible thing that Jesus described couldn't happen.

But not Peter. He was as defiant and as confident as he could be, and that's a dangerous combination. "Even if everyone else exits on You, Jesus, I'm here. I'm not goin' anywhere. I'm with You—all the way," Peter might have said with a bit of a Aramaic twang.

Peter Gives In to His Fear

Peter's actions ended up saying something entirely different from his words. The event is recorded in all four of the Gospels. You've probably read it before, but let's take a look at Matthew's account.

Now Peter was sitting out in the courtyard, and a servant girl came to him. "You also were with Jesus the Galilean," she said.

But he denied it before them all. "I don't know what you're talking about," he said.

Then he went out to the gateway, where another servant girl saw him and said to the people there, "This fellow was with Jesus of Nazareth."

He denied it again, with an oath: "I don't know the man!"

After a little while, those standing there went up to Peter and said, "Surely you are one of them; your accent gives you away."

Then he began to call down curses, and he swore to them, "I don't know the man!" Immediately a rooster crowed (Matthew 26:69-74 NIV).

What Jesus had said would happen, happened. No big surprise there. Peter did what he had told Jesus he would never do. He denied him not once, but three times. And he denied him not casually, but with words that would have to be bleeped off of a reality show if the cameras had been rolling.

Peter made the mistake of not realizing what he was capable of doing. He thought that denying Jesus was not in his character. He assumed that disloyalty wasn't in his character. He didn't think he could do something like that. But it was always in Peter's character to do it; he just didn't know it. Peter didn't think he could deny Jesus Christ, but as soon as the devil saw Peter was thinking that way, Satan decided that was exactly where he was going to target him.

That should serve as a warning to each of us. Satan often looks to bring us down in the very area where we would never imagine we could fall. When we know we're struggling, we usually have our guard up, or at least we're on the alert. But when, like Peter, we say that something like that could never happen to us, we need to be the most careful. Each one of us is capable of a lot more than we're often aware.

Throwing In the Towel

Following Peter's denial, we read that "he went out and wept bitterly." Crying like a baby, Peter had come face-to-face with the reality that he had done something he never thought he could do. Peter failed, and as a result, we see him returning to do the very thing he had left in order to follow Jesus. Peter gave up his life as a disciple, threw in the towel, and returned to where he had come from.

If you remember, in Luke 5:10-11, Jesus specifically called Peter away from his profession as a fisherman. "Jesus said to Simon, 'Do not fear, from now on you will be catching men.' When they had brought their boats to land, they left everything and followed Him."

Yet Peter had fallen, denying the One he had spent so much time with for three years. He pretended not to know the One whose power and person he had personally witnessed, and he headed back to what he had known before. He and several others went back to a life by the sea.

> Simon Peter, and Thomas called Didymus, and Nathanael of Cana in Galilee, and the sons of Zebedee, and two others of His disciples were together. Simon Peter said to them, "I am going fishing." They said to him, "We will also come with you." They went out and got into the boat; and that night they caught nothing (John 21:2-3).

Peter had left his old life behind to walk with Jesus. He had put down the bait, line, boat, and nets for Jesus. During those years, Peter got to witness miracle after miracle. People were raised from the dead. Blind people could see. The hungry were fed. What's more, Peter saw Jesus respond in love to those who hated Him and wanted Him dead. But despite all that he had witnessed, Peter went fishing again. He picked up the bait, line, boat, and nets once again to try his hand at what he thought he knew.

The problem was, Peter couldn't go back to how it was. He was out of sync and rusty. The passage tells us that he caught nothing. Peter was out on the boat all night long, and he experienced a rude awakening the next morning. His nets were empty, just as they had been the day he first met Jesus. I wonder if Peter got a feeling of familiarity that morning, thinking back to that moment when Jesus had instructed him to push his boat out into the deep waters and put down his nets. At the time, Peter hadn't known all that Jesus could do, and internally he had grumbled and complained at this carpenter presuming to tell him how to do his job.

But once the nets had become so full that they were about to make the boats sink, Peter had realized that something about this man, Jesus, was special. Whoever He was, He had a power unlike anything Peter had ever seen. It was a power from God, and Peter had wanted to experience more.

Three years later, Peter sat on an old, smelly boat once again—right where his story had begun. But this time he heard a voice calling to him from the shore. It sounded familiar, but it couldn't have been who he thought it was. He knew Jesus had risen from the grave—he and the other disciples had seen Him appear behind locked doors—but he didn't think Jesus would take the time to talk to him now. Peter had denied Jesus in the worst possible way on the worst possible night.

"Children, you do not have any fish, do you?" the voice called out to the men in the boat.

"No," the disciples answered.

"Cast the net on the right-hand side of the boat and you will find a catch," the voice called back to them (John 21:5-6). So they did, this time without a complaint or an argument. More than likely, they remembered how successful they had been three years earlier when they had followed the stranger's advice. And deep down inside, they were probably hopeful that this stranger wasn't a stranger at all. The Scripture records their response: "So they cast, and then they were not able to haul it in because of the great number of fish. Therefore that disciple whom Jesus loved said to Peter, 'It is the Lord'" (verses 6-7). Verse 11 tells us that there were 153 fish altogether. It was a massive catch after a long, fruitless night of trying to go back to what they had thought they could do.

Similar things happen to us as believers, I'm sure. Maybe after you fail in an area of your spiritual life, you decide it would be better if you just went back to what you knew once before. Maybe you go back to the old life, old crowd, or old club all night long. But just like Peter and the others, even after a long night, you catch nothing. You catch nothing because Jesus wants your eyes back on Him. He doesn't want to lose you after you've spent so much time with Him already. He loves you. Yes, maybe you fell away, just as Peter and the other biblical characters we're looking at in this book fell away, but Jesus longs for your return—so much so that He will show up where you least expect Him. That's what He did with Peter. And when He does, let your response to His love be no less enthusiastic than Peter's. "So when Simon Peter heard that it was the Lord, he put his outer garment on (for he was stripped for work), and threw himself into the sea" (verse 7).

Peter didn't waste any time getting to Jesus. Once Peter knew that Jesus was talking to him, Peter jumped in the water and swam to shore before the boat could get there. That's what forgiveness will do for you. Once you realize that Jesus still loves you and has forgiven you for what you've done, you'll desire to get to Him as fast as possible because that kind of love doesn't come around all that often. That love is filled with grace and filled with mercy.

When Peter got to the shore, breakfast was already cooking. "So when they got out on the land, they saw a charcoal fire already laid and fish placed on it, and bread" (verse 9). Why did John specifically say that the fish was cooking on top of a "charcoal fire"? That detail doesn't seem to be important, but John included it. Why?

The Greek word translated "charcoal" is only used twice in the entire New Testament. But what stands out about its use is that both times the word for "charcoal" is used, it's directly in relationship to Peter. The first time is in John 18:18: "Now the slaves and the officers were standing there, having made a charcoal fire, for it was cold and they were warming themselves; and Peter was also with them, standing and warming himself."

The first time we saw a reference to a charcoal fire, Peter was about to deny Jesus. The second time we read about a charcoal fire, Jesus has returned to forgive him. Jesus didn't want Peter to mentally set aside what he had done. When He sat down to have His conversation with Peter, He made sure that it took place in a very similar setting—a charcoal fire, like the one Peter stood beside when he denied Him. Jesus used a visual prop to emphasize His message.

From Peter to Simon

Not only that, but when we read further in the book of John, we discover that Peter experienced a verbal reminder in his conversation with Jesus as well. After they finished eating their breakfast, Jesus asked Peter three times if he loved Him. But if you look closely at the text, you will see that all three times, Jesus addressed Peter as Simon. "Simon, son of John, do you love Me?" Jesus repeated it three times—the same number of times that Peter had denied Him.

Earlier, in Matthew 16:17-19, we find Peter getting his name changed from Simon to Peter. This comes when Jesus is talking to the disciples about building His church and advancing God's kingdom. The name that Jesus gave to Simon (Peter) means "rock," and it served as a symbol of his leadership and significance in the church that Jesus would build.

However, once Peter denied Christ and went back to his old ways—fishing rather than being about the kingdom work Jesus had initiated—Jesus went back to calling him by the name Simon. If Peter was going to spend his days fishing for smelly perch rather than for men, Jesus was going to address him according to the name that fit what he was doing.

Jesus' reminders of Peter's denials included even more than the charcoal fire, the number of questions (three), and the name Simon. In addition, Jesus' questions centered on the area that Peter had once claimed so strongly: his love. Peter had told Jesus that even if everyone else fell away, he never would. He assured Jesus that his love was more loyal than anyone Jesus had ever known. Now that Peter's love had proven to be shallow, Jesus wanted to revisit that boast with him.

"Simon, son of John," Jesus asked him, "do you love Me?"

In these three exchanges between Jesus and Peter (John 21:15-19), it's critical to recognize the words translated "love." When Jesus asked Peter if he loved Him, Jesus used the Greek word *agape*, which signifies a loyal, committed, and self-sacrificing love. When Peter responded to Jesus' first question, he told Jesus that he loved Him, but he chose to use the Greek word *phileo*. *Phileo* could easily be translated "like." It's more indicative of a friendship than of a committed sacrifice.

Peter's response gave good reason to believe that he had learned his lesson. He wasn't about to put himself out there again, claiming that he could do something, be something, or love someone when he actually might not be able to. "I love You, Jesus," Peter replied. "But it's not the kind of love You're looking for."

Essentially, Jesus was asking Peter, "Do you love Me one hundred percent?" And Peter was replying, "No, I love You sixty-five percent." Peter didn't want to state anything more than what he knew to be true. He didn't want to risk being sifted like wheat all over again, so he didn't elevate himself as highly as he had before.

The second time Jesus asked Peter if he loved Him with *agape*, Peter answered again that he loved Him with *phileo*. Letting the point hit home, the third time Jesus asked Peter if he loved Him, He changed His question altogether and said, "Simon, do you *phileo* Me?" This deeply hurt Peter. "Peter was grieved because He said to him the third time, 'Do you love Me?'" The last time Peter had experienced a sequence of threes, the rooster had crowed, and Peter had run away and wept. This time the text says he was grieved.

The man who had so excitedly jumped into the water to swim to Jesus had been brought right back to his point of departure. The charcoal fire burned, the name reflected the vocation, the question had been asked three times, and committed love had been reduced to friendship. Jesus had taken Peter right back to his mess, and when Peter realized the connection, his heart tore in two.

Peter's response to Jesus after the third question intensified. Earlier he had replied, "Yes, Lord, You know..." But this time, Peter said, "Lord, You know all things." Peter had intimated that Jesus obviously didn't know what He was talking about when He told Peter that he would deny Him. But now Peter tells Jesus, "You know all things." Peter now knew that Jesus knew him better than he knew himself.

Each of us can learn a valuable lesson from Peter. One of the problems we often face as believers is that we really don't believe God knows us better than we know ourselves. Sometimes we think we're fooling God. We dress up for church, quote our verses, put on our Sunday attitude, say the right things, and do what good Christians are supposed to do, but God knows who we really are when we gather around the charcoal fires of life. He knows that even though we talk a good game, most of us would be flying high just to love Him 65 percent.

And just as it broke Peter's heart to realize that he wasn't all that he had thought he was—that Jesus had to come down to his 65 percent by changing *agape* to *phileo* in His question—it should break our hearts to realize we aren't all we think we are either. It might be easy to be the heroic Christian when things are going well, but when

Satan knows the right buttons to push on you and he asks permission to sift you like wheat, only Jesus knows what you will really do. Many of us have learned that answer too—the hard way.

But the good thing is that Jesus will come down to our 65 percent and meet us where we are. And when He does, He will still give us a purpose that's beyond ourselves, just as He did with Peter. Jesus gave Peter's job back to him. He gave his mission back to him. He said, "Peter, tend My lambs." In other words, "Peter—take care of those who are following Me. I told you that you would be a fisher of men, and I am still going to make you exactly what I said you would be. Your job is secure despite your failure. Peter, I want you to take care of those whom I care about deeply—My sheep."

Peter had just experienced a true comeback. Because of his setback and restoration, he was now more able to take care of others who might be struggling and hurting too. Now he could identify with them and rely on God to help him do what he needed to do. God could use Peter at an even greater level now because Peter wasn't just going to be spouting theology and patting his own back any longer. Peter knew how it felt to fail, hurt, and need another chance. Peter knew how to strengthen others who were in a similar place by helping them to see the same Jesus who met him at his point of failure.

I imagine if Peter lived today, many people wouldn't allow him to preach in their pulpits. Many people in Christendom would scoff at a rebound like this. They wouldn't let him teach at their conferences or their Sunday school classes, write books for their church members, or even sing songs about Him. But Jesus would. In fact, Jesus put Peter straight to work taking care of those He cared about the most—His own. Jesus says, "Peter, if all you can do right now is *phileo* Me, then that's good enough. I'll take it. We'll start with the sixty-five percent, and we'll go from there."

The key qualification for God to use you is that you're honest about your love for Him. But how do you know you love someone? It's not by a tingly feeling you get inside. The way to tell whether you love someone is by looking at what you *do*. Anyone can say, "I love you." But the people who really love you care about what's important to you. They have your best interest in mind. If people tell you they love you, but every decision in their lives seems to be all about them, they don't love you. They are just using the words for their own benefit. To love someone is to make what is important to them a priority to you.

Jesus knows we love Him when He sees us caring about the things He cares about—His sheep. Scripture tells us, "If someone says, 'I love God,' and hates his brother, he is a liar; for the one who does not love his brother whom he has seen, cannot love God whom he has not seen" (1 John 4:20).

By asking Peter to tend to His sheep, Jesus restored Peter to public service. Peter had committed a public sin—he had dismissed and denied Jesus publicly. So Jesus restored Peter publicly as well, in front of the other disciples. As a result, Peter received Christ's forgiveness, and that became the foundation for everything that he would do as he moved forward.

God Knows the Worst and the Best

Peter's story is a great example of public affirmation after a public failure. But what does Peter's story have to do with us? One thing we see through Peter's story is that God knows the worst about each of us even before we do it. He knows what is in our closets and gutters and what's stuffed underneath our beds. Those things you think no one else knows about you…God knows them all. And God wants to make sure you know about them too. Or do you still think you could never fall? That's a dangerous thought to have.

Likewise, even though God knows the worst there is to know about you, He also knows the best there is to know about you. And He wants to use you to strengthen others, just as He used Peter. He knows that once you have rebounded from your failures, you have the potential to be stronger than you were before your failure. The scared, shaking-in-his-boots Peter who denied Jesus in His hour of need is the same bold and confident Peter who stood up to proclaim Jesus' name at Pentecost, ushering more than 3000 people into the kingdom in one day. In the era of Billy Graham-sized crusades, we may think that the number 3000 isn't that impressive. But in biblical days and in biblical culture, Peter was used by God in the largest recorded response to the gospel of Jesus Christ. In addition, this event ushered in the church age that we know today.

And beyond even that, Peter was used to bring Gentiles into the church, as we see later in his ministry to an influential Gentile man named Cornelius (Acts 10). Once Peter became honest and acknowledged the deficits inside of him, he also became useful and powerful in the kingdom. He admitted that 65 percent was all that he had to give on his own, but God made up the difference over the rest of his life, and Peter ended up giving all 100 percent of himself to the kingdom.

If you have ever failed God, denied Him, dismissed Him, doubted Him, ignored Him, or just plain left Him, and if, like Peter, you have a sign on your heart that says you have gone fishing, I want you to listen for the familiar voice that Peter heard that morning. That same voice is calling to you as well.

If you will answer Him and return to Him, He can use you in ways you could never imagine. It is not too late. Rather, it's the perfect time to have some breakfast with Jesus. It's the perfect time to come clean before Him. You might as well—He has known the truth about you all along. Maybe you didn't, but He did. And now that you know it too, you're in an even greater position for Him to be able to use you.

Will you answer His call? I imagine that you might be a lot like Peter right now and that you haven't caught much in a long time on your own. So what do you have to lose?

He is waiting for you. You have a job to do.

7

Samson Was a Player

S amson was a player. He was a lady's man. In fact, Samson loved
the women so much that one woman in particular, Delilah,
would prove to be his downfall. Despite everything Samson had
going for him, he lacked the strength to resist her.

Samson was smart, strong, handsome, confident, and anointed.
He rose to be a leader over Israel for 20 years. Yet despite all that and
more, Samson had one weakness: women.

If you've read the four chapters in Judges that cover the life of
Samson, you might wonder why I would choose to include him in
a book like this. Or you could wonder why God chose to include
Samson in the Hall of Faith in Hebrews 11 with heroes like Abraham, Moses, and Joseph. When you read Samson's story, you could
be tempted to think he doesn't belong there. You may even wonder
what he's doing in the Bible at all. But he is there—as big as life—
and he's included among the great men and women of faith.

As far as faith goes, you could say that Samson was born with a silver spoon of anointing. We're introduced to him in the book of Judges when the angel of the Lord speaks to his mother.

> You are barren and childless, but you are going to become pregnant and give birth to a son. Now see to it that you drink no wine or other fermented drink and that you do not eat anything unclean. You will become pregnant and have a son whose head is never to be touched by a razor because the boy is to be a Nazirite, dedicated to God from the womb. He will take the lead in delivering Israel from the hands of the Philistines (Judges 13:3-5 NIV).

The angel of the Lord appeared to Samson's mother and told her that the son she was about to have would be "dedicated to God from the womb." He would be a Nazirite. A Nazirite was an Israelite who had taken a special vow of dedication to God. In his vow, the Nazirite was to do three specific things. First, he was to abstain from wine.

> He shall abstain from wine and strong drink; he shall drink no vinegar, whether made from wine or strong drink, nor shall he drink any grape juice nor eat fresh or dried grapes. All the days of his separation he shall not eat anything that is produced by the grape vine, from the seeds even to the skin (Numbers 6:3-4).

Repeatedly in the Old Testament, wine or grape juice is a type, or symbol, indicating joy or gladness. As part of the vow, a Nazirite was to willingly abstain from this particular thing that could bring him much pleasure. This is similar to Christ's command to believers: "If anyone wishes to come after Me, he must deny himself, and take up his cross daily and follow Me" (Luke 9:23). A Nazirite was to forego certain pleasures as part of his dedication to God.

Second, a Nazirite was not to cut his hair. "All the days of his vow of separation no razor shall pass over his head. He shall be holy until the days are fulfilled for which he separated himself to the LORD; he shall let the locks of hair on his head grow long" (Numbers 6:5).

As Paul writes in the New Testament, long hair for a man was seen as a disgrace. He says, "Does not even nature itself teach you that if a man has long hair, it is a dishonor to him?" (1 Corinthians 11:14). A Nazirite's willingness to wear his hair long in a culture that didn't respect that attribute in a man was an outward indication of his dedication and his ability to overcome his own pride. True commitment is seen not only in a people's devotion but also in their ability to harness their own conceit into a willing humility.

Lastly, a Nazirite was not to come into contact with a dead body.

> All the days of his separation to the LORD he shall not go near to a dead person. He shall not make himself unclean for his father or for his mother, for his brother or for his sister, when they die, because his separation to God is on his head. All the days of his separation he is holy to the LORD (Numbers 6:6-8).

Not coming near a dead person meant much more than we might first think. The command went into great detail, including the father, mother, brother, or sister, so this vow prohibited the Nazirite from experiencing a cultural tradition of grieving the closest of kin who had died. But through this separation to God, the Nazirite learned how to avoid worldly entanglements and keep an eternal perspective. Jesus gave a similar command to an aspiring disciple when He said, "Follow Me, and allow the dead to bury their own dead" (Matthew 8:22).

A Nazirite vow covered a number of areas of great importance in life. Because it was so all-encompassing, most often it would be chosen by the Nazirite himself. But in the case of Samson, his dedication was decided before he was even born. He was to be uniquely set apart for God to "begin to deliver Israel from the hands of the Philistines" (Judges 13:5).

You can tell a lot about Samson simply by his name. Samson is a man's name that rolls off of your tongue and resounds with strength. This was a man who definitely "had it going on." Even today Samson is known as a herculean figure in the annals of history—a man who could pull off superhuman feats, even without changing into tights and a cape. Samson had Harrison Ford's skills and Bruce Willis' daring. He was as strong as Sylvester Stallone and as debonair as Denzel Washington.

Samson was every man's nightmare and every woman's dream.

Being a man like that, it would be easy for Samson to get a big head. But Samson heard one thing over and over again as he was growing up—his strengths belonged to God.

His mother would have reminded him frequently that even his birth was supernatural. After all, she couldn't have children. She was barren. But God supernaturally touched her womb, allowing her to conceive and give birth to a child with a great purpose. Samson's purpose was to deliver Israel from their oppression. In other words, Samson was under contract to play for the Kingdom Nazirites, and his divine assignment was to sack, tackle, and intercept the Philistine Warriors.

Speaking of football, longtime Pittsburgh Steelers safety Troy Polamalu, who recently grabbed the AP Defensive Player of the Year award, has something in common with Samson. Polamalu is probably even more famous for his hair than for playing football. When the black-and-gold take the field, one player stands out more than any other, and that is Polamalu. As he tackles ball carriers, sacks quarterbacks, and breaks up or intercepts passes, Polamalu is instantly recognized by his long black mane flowing freely from underneath his helmet. Polamalu's hair is so valuable that Procter & Gamble insured it for $1 million. (Polamalu has a contract with Procter & Gamble to endorse Head & Shoulders shampoo.)

Samson would have done well to recognize the value of his hair too. When Samson lost his hair, he lost everything.

Supernatural Spiritual Power

Yet before we jump ahead to Samson's barbershop visit, let's take a look at his life. When reading about Samson's life, we often see the Spirit of the Lord coming upon him. We first read about this shortly after we're told of Samson's birth: "The child grew up and the LORD blessed him. And the Spirit of the LORD began to stir him" (Judges 13:24-25).

We later read that the "Spirit of the LORD came upon him mightily so that he tore [a lion] as one tears a young goat though he had nothing in his hand" (Judges 14:6).

And in Judges 15:14 we read that "the Spirit of the LORD came upon him mightily so that the ropes that were on his arms were as flax that is burned with fire." Samson then grabbed the jawbone of a donkey and proceeded to kill a thousand men with it.

Throughout Samson's life, it was evident that his calling to be a Nazirite gave him access to a greater spiritual power than was humanly possible. Samson had power when he confronted his enemies—both human and animal—because God's Spirit came upon him in those times.

It's important for us to note that every believer in the church age has access to the same Spirit that empowered Samson. God may not be calling us to adhere to the same Nazirite vows, but we are called to live lives that are sanctified (set apart for God). When our lives are set apart from the world's standards and we devote ourselves to God, His Spirit empowers us to face our enemies of self-doubt, stressful relationships, difficult job situations, and even health problems. Yet like Samson, if we lose our uniqueness as children of God who are set apart to Him to live holy lives, we lose our power.

Today we see a generation of powerless Christians simply because we're not living sanctified lives. It's as if we're messing with our Nazirite vows either by merging our thoughts and viewpoints with the world's or by making poor choices about how we spend our time or what company we keep and for what reasons. Even our physical ability to think clearly, function well, or live with vitality and strength is compromised when we eat the wrong foods on a regular basis or eat too much. These actions can affect the amount of energy, desire, and zeal we have for God and for life itself. If we're not taking care of our bodies and we're filling ourselves with tasty treats that simply weigh us down emotionally and physically, we're not setting ourselves apart for God. We're not viewing our bodies as His temples and managing them accordingly.

It's important to realize that Samson didn't just wake up one day with his head in Delilah's lap and his hair being shaved. Samson lost his power because his life story was marked with compromise. We too can end up in a place we never imagined possible when we compromise smaller things and make choices that don't reflect a life set apart to serve and glorify God. Samson's first compromise began with his choice of a bride.

> Samson went down to Timnah and saw a woman in Timnah, one of the daughters of the Philistines. So he came back and told his father and mother, "I saw a woman in Timnah, one of the daughters of the Philistines; now therefore, get her for me as a wife" (Judges 14:1-2).

Samson saw a woman and decided he wanted to marry her. The only problem was that this woman was from the enemy. She was a Philistine. Not only that, but God had made it clear that the Israelites were not to marry pagans. To do so was the same as establishing a covenant with another god.

Marriage is a covenant. From a spiritual standpoint, it goes much deeper than just two people living with each other and possibly raising some kids. As Paul exhorts us, "Do not be yoked together with unbelievers. For what do righteousness and wickedness have in common? Or what fellowship can light have with darkness?" (2 Corinthians 6:14 NIV). The reason for this distinction in marriage is that the marriage covenant is much more than a contract; it is a joining of two people *spiritually*.

Another reason believers are experiencing so much powerlessness is that we've gone from being *in* the world to being *of* the world. Scripture tells us we're to be in the world but not of the world. This can be compared to a boat being in the water without the water being in the boat. If the water were to get in the boat, the boat would sink. God isn't calling us to be hermits or monks when He calls us to be set apart, but He *is* calling us to live in the world without letting the world be in us.

When we try to mix worldly standards with God's values, we end up alienating ourselves from the one true God and losing His presence and His power in our lives, just as Samson did. Samson didn't immediately lose his power by marrying the Philistine woman, but his compromise started him down a path of even greater compromises that ultimately ended in his destruction.

Yet he saw a woman who looked beautiful—or as we might say, oh so fine—and told his parents he wanted to marry her. He didn't care that she was an enemy and that God had said not to marry foreigners. He didn't care that his parents advised him not to do it. All Samson knew was that the girl looked good to him, so he told his parents once again, "Get her for me" (Judges 14:3).

Riddles in His Role

Samson is a player. He's a tease. All through these four chapters covering his life in the Bible, we see Samson playing around with women, making jokes, or saying riddles. Samson must have learned early on that he was a girl-magnet because he bounced from one girl to another. In fact, his first wife—the Philistine—didn't get to hang around too long at all. She betrayed Samson's trust by convincing him to tell her the answer to his riddle and then telling her family the answer, and Samson responded in anger. His wife's father, trying to protect her, gave her to another companion instead, but when Samson returned for her and discovered that he couldn't have her, he set out on a jealous rampage of revenge.

Samson caught 300 foxes, tied them tail to tail, and fastened a torch to each pair of tails. The he released them into Philistine farmland. When the Philistines saw their grain and vineyards burning up, they asked who started the fires. Learning that Samson had targeted them out of anger for his Philistine wife, the Philistines turned against their own people and burned both Samson's wife and her father.

This, of course, made Samson even angrier. He slaughtered many Philistines for what they had done and went to live in a cave at Etam. When the Philistines came after him, Samson was once again given power from on high, and he single-handedly struck down 1000 Philistines.

The next 20 years of Samson's life have not been recorded for us in the Bible, but I would be surprised if they didn't contain the same level of intrigue, suspense, conflict, and power that we have seen so far. Even though we aren't told much about those years, we do know that Samson fulfilled his role as judge over Israel, just as he had been created to do. We read, "He judged Israel twenty years in the days of the Philistines" (Judges 15:20).

When we meet Samson again some 20 years later, we find him up to his same old routine. Here we discover Samson fraternizing with a hooker, putting him at great risk of personal exposure.

> Now Samson went to Gaza and saw a harlot there, and went in to her. When it was told to the Gazites, saying, "Samson has come here," they surrounded the place and lay in wait for him all night at the gate of the city. And

they kept silent all night, saying, "Let us wait until the
morning light, then we will kill him." Now Samson lay
until midnight, and at midnight he arose and took hold
of the doors of the city gate and the two posts and pulled
them up along with the bars; then he put them on this
shoulders and carried them up to the top of the mountain which is opposite Hebron (Judges 16:1-3).

The Philistines had discovered that Samson was hanging out in
their red-light district, so they had arranged a strategy to destroy
him. The problem was that Samson's strength was more than they
had bargained for. At midnight, Samson yanked the doors of the
city gate clear out of the ground. These gates weren't similar to what
you might have in your backyard. They were enormous gates that
caravans could pass through. It wasn't humanly possible for Samson to pull up those gates and carry them 40 miles to the top of the
mountain, making the entire city vulnerable to attack. But Samson's power was not found in human strength. It was found in God
because He had chosen Samson to fulfill a specific purpose at a specific time—to lead the Israelites in their deliverance from the Philistines.

Samson's power came from God. As we have already seen, Samson was chosen before he was born. His calling obviously wasn't the
result of anything he had done, yet he was empowered to honor God
by leading His people out of an oppressive situation. Nevertheless,
Samson's empowerment was conditional. It was contingent upon
Samson keeping his Nazarite vows. Unfortunately, Samson met a
woman who would prove to be even more powerful than he was.
That woman's name was Delilah.

As is common with names in the Bible, Delilah's name tells us
a lot about her. It may even give us a hint as to why Samson fell so
deeply in love with her. The name Delilah literally means "delicate"
or "soft." There is no question that Delilah was a beautiful woman

who offered Samson the exact opposite of his own rugged frame. Yet Delilah may have possessed more than mere beauty, because the Scripture tells us that Samson "loved a woman in the valley of Sorek, whose name was Delilah" (verse 4).

Frequently in the Bible when we read about a man's attraction to a woman's beauty, she will be described as beautiful, or attractive in form. No such words are given to Delilah, although her name alone offers us an idea of her appearance. Yet the hold Delilah had over Samson may have gone deeper than just what he saw, because we read that Samson loved Delilah. He was smitten by her—besotted. Infatuated. Love struck.

How else can we explain how Delilah pulled off what thousands of determined Philistine men could never do? How else can we understand how Delilah could ask Samson not once, twice, or even three times, but four times for the secret to his amazing strength without him packing his bags and leaving this far-too-inquisitive woman? Samson loved Delilah, and ultimately the player got played.

Playing the Player

When the Philistines discovered that Samson had fallen for Delilah, they approached Delilah to make her a deal. They offered to pay her handsomely for betraying Samson.

> The lords of the Philistines came up to her and said to her, "Entice him, and see where his great strength lies and how we may overpower him that we may bind him to afflict him. Then we will each give you eleven hundred pieces of silver" (verse 5).

The passage doesn't tell us how many Philistine lords approached Delilah. But however many there were, each one agreed to pay her an enormous amount of money to turn Samson's secret over to them.

For 20 years, Samson had defended, judged, and led the Israelites in the face of the Philistine oppression. The Philistines were undoubtedly tired of going up against an enemy who somehow embodied superhuman strength.

Enticing Delilah to work her magic over her man, the Philistines set a plan in motion to capture their nemesis. After all, Samson loved Delilah, and when a man loves a woman, she can get him to do things he never even dreamed he would do. And that's exactly what Delilah did because as it turned out, she was a gold digger.

Following an evening together, Delilah asked Samson to tell her the source of his strength. Samson, always a lover of riddles and jokes, told Delilah he would become weak if he was bound with seven fresh cords. Delilah, unaware that Samson had lied to her, bound him with seven fresh cords and called the Philistines to come and subdue him. Because Samson had lied, he broke through the cords as if they were nothing more than paper.

Delilah, obviously disappointed, tried again. This time Samson told her he would become weak if he was bound with new ropes. So after Samson fell asleep, Delilah did just that. However, when she called for the Philistines to attack him, Samson broke through the new ropes just as he had the fresh cords.

A third time Delilah urged Samson to tell her his secret. This time Samson told Delilah part of the truth (he talked about his hair) but not the whole truth. He simply said that if the seven locks of his hair were woven with the web, he would lose his strength.

After he had fallen asleep, Delilah went to work on Samson's hair, weaving it and pinning it just as he had said. Yelling that the Philistines were upon him for a third time, Samson broke free and revealed to Delilah that he had deceived her once again.

Finally, frustrated, Delilah tried something new. Calling upon his obvious love for her, she said, "How can you say, 'I love you,' when your heart is not with me? You have deceived me these three times and have not told me where your great strength is" (verse 15).

Delilah played the love card. "You don't really love me, Samson. You've never loved me," Delilah pouted. "If you did, you would answer my question and stop lying to me." At first, Delilah still didn't get the response she wanted, even with the love card. But 1100 pieces of silver from each Philistine lord urged her to continue. So she kept asking, kept asking, and kept asking Samson.

> It came about when she pressed him daily with her words and urged him, that his soul was annoyed to death. So he told her all that was in his heart and said to her, "A razor has never come on my head, for I have been a Nazirite to God from my mother's womb. If I am shaved, then my strength will leave me and I will become weak and be like any other man" (verses 16-17).

Basically, Delilah nagged Samson. That's what "she pressed him daily" means in today's language. Delilah refused to take no for an answer and started in on Samson day in and day out. Any man who has a woman nagging him is in for a very long day. Proverbs 21:9 says plainly, "It is better to live in a corner of a roof than in a house shared with a contentious woman." Not only that, we also read in Proverbs 19:3 (NIV), "A quarrelsome wife is like a constant dripping of a leaky roof." Drip, drip, drip, drip, and drip.

Delicate, lovely, soft Delilah had become a dripping faucet—so much so that she frayed Samson's last nerve. She drove him nuts. We read that Samson's "soul was annoyed to death." That's pretty severe. Samson was ready to jump off a cliff. So to get Delilah to stop nagging, Samson told her his secret. She had worn him down, and Samson finally gave in.

Now aware of Samson's secret, Delilah took the next step toward her goal of retiring early and living a life of luxury. She called the lords of the Philistines and told them that this time she knew Samson had told her the truth. "Bring your money with you," she said, "because this time it's going to work." We read, "Then the lords of the Philistines came up to her and brought the money in their hands" (verse 18).

After Delilah saw that the money was there, she went ahead with the next step in her plan. To ensure that Samson would not wake up while his head was being shaved, Delilah went about the business of wearing him out. I won't go into details, but there is one sure way of wearing a man out, and the Bible alludes to this in the next verse: "She made him sleep on her knees" (verse 19). Apparently Samson and Delilah had a wild night at the crib.

After Samson fell asleep, Delilah called for help shaving off the seven locks of his hair. Then, to test him first herself, Delilah "began to afflict him," and Samson's "strength left him"—not because his strength was located in his hair, but because his hair was the symbol of his vow of devotion to God. When his Nazirite vow was intact, the Spirit of the Lord would come upon Samson and empower him. When it was broken, Samson was left to his own strength, and even Delilah could afflict him. When Samson lost his hair, he lost his vow, which meant he was no longer functioning according to his calling.

Samson's story is a reminder for each of us. God has created each one of us with a purpose to fulfill. You can call it your destiny or your calling. But when you choose to operate outside of your calling, you are operating outside of God's power. When you step outside of the uniqueness that God has created you for, you have placed yourself outside of where the power of the Spirit flows. You don't lose the Holy Spirit, but you do lose His power and presence at the level you would have were you walking within your purpose.

However, when you're living according to the calling God has designed you for, you will find power to do things you never could have done on your own. His Spirit will come upon you and enable you to be more than you could ever be on your own. That's called living in the sweet spot. It's living according to His strength and not your own.

But Samson left the sweet spot for something he thought was

sweeter, and as a result, he lost everything. "The Philistines are upon you, Samson!" Delilah yelled.

> And he awoke from his sleep and said, "I will go out as at other times and shake myself free." But he did not know that the LORD had departed from him. Then the Philistines seized him and gouged out his eyes; and they brought him down to Gaza and bound him with bronze chains, and he was a grinder in the prison (verses 20-21).

It can't get much worse than that. The Philistines dragged Samson to Gaza after having gouged out his eyes, and then they put him to work like an ox grinding grain—all because Samson chose not to remain separate and unique as a Nazarite. He revealed the source of his strength to a woman he loved even though she had already shown herself to be untrustworthy. And so the Spirit did not come upon Samson that day, just as the Spirit doesn't always come upon us even though we may be at church acting the right way and saying the right things. The Spirit is not required to provide us with His power and presence just because we request it. God says He wants us to be set apart to Him in our lives, and when we are set apart, that's when we discover all He has in store for us.

One passage that makes this principle clear to us in the church age is 1 John 2:15: "Do not love the world nor the things in the world. If anyone loves the world, the love of the Father is not in him." John didn't say we're not to be in the world. He just said don't be in love with it. Don't give the world the value and attachment that belongs to God.

Keep in mind that the world is essentially anything that leaves God out. It's anything that God cannot be a part of. The world is anything that makes you say, "God, You stay over here while I go over there. When I come back out, I'll pick You back up again." That is loving the world. It's embracing any viewpoint or activity that's not aligned underneath the overarching rule of God's kingdom agenda.

John instructs us not to love the world because if we do, we will lose the power of the Father. It's the same thing that happened with Samson. Samson sacrificed the Spirit's power for a fleshly urge. We too sacrifice the power of God in our own lives when we choose to align our lives with the world's standards, goals, ideals, and purposes rather than with God's. You can be in the world. In fact, you should be in the world. It's just that the world should not be in you. That's when you start to lose God's supernatural power in your life.

Redemption at the End

When Samson lost his power, his enemies began to gloat. This was the man who had killed 1000 of their people with nothing more than his bare hands and a donkey's jawbone. And now he was grinding their grain. In fact, the grain Samson was grinding was a continual reminder that he was now using his strength for a false god—Dagon was the Philistines' god of grain. Samson spent his time and energy in the service of the Philistines' false god. All the while, the Philistines celebrated their victory.

> Now the lords of the Philistines assembled to offer a great sacrifice to Dagon their god, and to rejoice, for they said, "Our god has given Samson our enemy into our hands." When the people saw him, they praised their god, for they said, "Our god has given our enemy into our hands, even the destroyer of our country, who has slain many of us" (Judges 16:23-24).

Samson is blind, bound, and grinding grain amid the cheers and praises of his captors. The enemy is now telling the player what game he is going to play. The enemy is calling the shots, and Samson doesn't have a choice but to follow. Once a person becomes blind and bound, nothing but God can get him out of that situation. And at that point, because he had broken his vow, God's power had left him.

Thankfully though, God is a gracious God. That's why Samson stands out among many as a reminder that regardless of what you may have done, how far you may have drifted, or how long you may have been gone, if you will reconnect with God, He has a plan for you. We read that eventually, "the hair of his head began to grow again after it was shaved off" (verse 22). Let's call it Miracle Grow, but in time, Samson started to get his groove back. Even though he had broken his vow and lost his power, God renewed His presence with him by having Samson's hair grow back as it was before.

Sin had led to the cutting of Samson's hair. Yet while the Philistines were busy partying with their god, and as Samson was grinding the grain in his prison, Samson's hair had started growing back. What Samson had lost because of sin, he was now getting back because he had repented of his sin. You can regain what you have lost because of sin only when you repent of that sin.

If you're seeking God and asking Him to restore your peace, restore your joy, or even restore your hope, and you can't seem to see any solution…if, like Samson, you have become blind to the solution and are now bound in your consequences, I urge you to agree with God about where you may have gone wrong in your life and ask Him to enable you to get back on the right road. That's called repentance. That's one way God turns things around, as we will see with Samson.

The Curtain Call

While the Philistines were celebrating their victory over Samson, they decided to put him on display.

> While they were in high spirits, they shouted, "Bring out Samson to entertain us." So they called Samson out of the prison, and he performed for them…
> Now the temple was crowded with men and women;

all the rulers of the Philistines were there, and on the roof were about three thousand men and women watching Samson perform (verses 25,27 NIV).

Samson had been dragged out into public to become the laughingstock to upward of 10,000 people. If 3000 alone were on the roof and the roof (most likely the overflow), then a number far greater than that would be at the party inside the building. Until that time, Samson had killed approximately 1000 of his enemies. Yet now he was surrounded by close to 10,000 of his enemies. Recognizing the unique position he was in, and knowing his hair had grown back, Samson made one last request.

> Then Samson prayed to the LORD, "Sovereign LORD, remember me. Please, God, strengthen me just once more, and let me with one blow get revenge on the Philistines for my two eyes." Then Samson reached toward the two central pillars on which the temple stood. Bracing himself against them, his right hand on the one and his left hand on the other, Samson said, "Let me die with the Philistines!" Then he pushed with all his might, and down came the temple on the rulers and all the people in it. Thus he killed many more when he died than while he lived (verses 28-30 NIV).

At Samson's death, he did more than he had done in 20 years of serving as judge over Israel. When all appeared to be lost for Samson and he stood blind, bound, and weak while grinding grain for a false god, Samson ended up accomplishing more than in any of the years he lived at full strength. This is because God has a way of redeeming what has been lost if you will let Him.

Just as the final two minutes of a football game will often be when the winner or loser is determined, the latter part of your life is a critical time period for claiming your own victory. Regardless of what mistakes or detours you've made, when you get right with God, God can do more amazing things in you and through you in the final moments of life than He did throughout the rest of your life. It's never too late with God.

Samson ended up in the Hebrews 11 Hall of Faith as a great man of faith because in spite of his failures, He looked to God to fulfill His purpose in faith.

Friend, you may be bound, blind, and feeling defeated, but your latter days can be greater than your former days. Look to God in the midst of your mess and call on Him to restore the purpose you were made to fulfill. Samson may seem like an odd person to read about in a chapter on faith, but believing isn't as much about living a life of perfection as it is about trusting God to use you even when you might be broken.

In spite of his failures, Samson fulfilled the calling God had placed on his life, which should give us all hope that God is bigger than our mistakes, and He can still use us in spite of us.

8

Sarah Was a Doubter

Sarah was a doubter. And her story is unlike the others—that's why I've saved her for last. Sarah's name literally means "princess." She had a lot going for her. Sarah had married a successful man named Abraham who had wealth, honor, and influence. In fact, if there had been a reality show called *The Real Housewives of Canaan*, Sarah would have been a member of the cast.

Yet even though Sarah had a lot of great things going in her favor, one major element was missing from her life. Sarah was barren. In all of her years with Abraham, she had never experienced the joy of becoming pregnant and having a child.

Being unable to have a child was one of the worst things that could happen to a woman in Sarah's time and culture. Being childless carried a stigma of being under a curse. Despite all of the things that were going well for Sarah, her inability to conceive, incubate, and deliver new life had cast a dark shadow over her life.

Sarah's physical reality that we read about in the Old Testament is a lot of people's spiritual reality in the world we live in today. They may have a lot of things going for them—a successful career, a happy family, attractive looks, or a stockpile of material goods—but the ability to house the abundant life we've been given through Jesus Christ isn't there. Instead, they live each day with a perpetual empty nagging inside that knocks at the door of a heart that has learned how to exist rather than to thrive.

They lack the capacity to have, hold, incubate, and celebrate life within themselves or with others. Going through the routine and the motions, their lives feel barren, stale, and lonely.

Barrenness can lend itself to many other ills. It can lead to hopelessness, depression, and doubt. String together enough days, weeks, or even years of barrenness, and a person can pretty much conclude that nothing is ever going to change. Most likely, that's how Sarah felt at the age of 65 without having yet given birth to a child. I'm not a medical doctor, but I assume that if a woman hasn't given birth by the time she's 65 years old, she never will.

Unfortunately, Sarah assumed the same thing. And because she did, she failed to fully enjoy God's promise when He made it. Instead, she laughed in disbelief.

Sarah was a doubter. But the interesting thing is that even though Sarah was a doubter, she still somehow ended up smack dab in the middle of the Hall of Faith in Hebrews 11.

Barrenness as a Lifestyle

But before we dive too quickly into Sarah's story, I want to talk about you. We have dropped in on a number of people so far in our time together. We've taken a look at Moses the murderer, Rahab the harlot, Jacob, Jonah, Peter, Samson...and who could forget Esther the diva? We've seen how God redeemed situations, people, decisions, and personalities, manifesting His glory in and through them.

But of all of the people we've looked at so far, I have a hunch that Sarah might be the one you will identify with the most. You may not be struggling with the same kind of barrenness that Sarah faced, but I have a feeling that if you picked up this book, you might be facing your own spiritual desert of sorts. Maybe you're living in an extended period of time in which the *life* seems to have gone missing from your life.

Perhaps you feel lonely because you are relationally barren. Or perhaps you feel defeated because you haven't yet reached your professional or personal goals. You lack productivity, drive, focus, or ambition. But more than that, you lack *hope*. It could be that you've even forgotten what it means to have a dream.

I challenged our Wednesday evening congregation a while ago to pursue the dream that God had placed within each of them. One of our members confided in me later that life had been so barren for so long, even if there once was a dream, it was now long gone—unable to even be recalled. Maybe you feel like this person. You can't imagine what Jesus is referring to when He says that He has come to give you *abundant* life.

A beautiful illustration of abundant life walked into my office not too long ago. Both she and her husband came in just days before she was scheduled to give birth. Now, I have seen many pregnant women over the years around our church, but I have rarely seen anyone this pregnant. She couldn't even walk. All she could do was waddle, rocking from side to side. I asked her how things were going with the baby, and her response explained everything.

"There's not just one baby in here," she said. "There are two."

No wonder she had become so consumed with the life she was carrying. This lady wasn't just carrying one life—she was carrying *abundant* life. This is exactly what Jesus says He came to give to each of us. The life Christ gives has the capacity to take over every area of your being. It can even change the way you walk. And yet many of us still walk around empty inside, as barren as Sarah.

When the Promise Delays

Before God's promise could come to fruition in Sarah's life, she had to pass through a time of conflicted emptiness. Can you relate with her? Sarah's emptiness was conflicted because she knew that God had promised her husband that He was going to make him a great nation. Yet God made that promise when Abraham, then called Abram, was 75 and Sarah, then called Sarai, was 65.

> Go forth from your country,
>   And from your relatives
>   And from your father's house,
>   To the land which I will show you;
> and I will make you a great nation,
>   and I will bless you,
>   and make your name great;
>   and so you shall be a blessing;
> And I will bless those who bless you,
>   and the one who curses you I will curse,
>   and in you all the families of the earth will be blessed
>   (Genesis 12:1-3).

God pronounced a blessing on Abraham. He promised him that through him, God was going to do something very special for the entire world. He said that He was going to make Abraham a great nation. But in order to become a great nation, Abraham first needed a son. Yet at 75 and 65 years old, Abraham and Sarah weren't just old—at this point, they were cold. Even so, God told Abraham that in the middle of their barrenness, He was going to give them life.

At first, Abraham was confused, so he struck up a conversation with God to try to sort things out. Abraham understood the promise—that he was going to be a great nation—but at his age, he didn't quite understand the process.

> "O Lord GOD, what will you give me, since I am child-
> less, and the heir of my house is Eliezer of Damascus?"
> And Abram said, "Since You have given no offspring to
> me, one born in my house is my heir" (Genesis 15:2-3).

But God had other plans because God is not confined to the ways
of man.

> "This man will not be your heir; but one who will come
> forth from your own body, he shall be your heir." And
> He took him outside and said, "Now look toward the
> heavens, and count the stars, if you are able to count
> them." And He said to him, "So shall your descendants
> be" (verses 4-5).

When Sarah found out about this promise, she concluded that
God must not know much about biology. Maybe He's confused,
she assumed. Maybe He's lost contact with the way things work on
earth. Sarah realized that if a woman had been barren all her life, and
she was now 65 years old, she was not going to have a baby. Things
just didn't happen that way.

So Sarah did what many of us often do—she tried to help God
out. She believed His promise, or at least she believed that He had
good intentions about His promise. But then Sarah took it upon herself to force that promise into reality. She came up with her own plan
to bring about God's plan because she thought that God couldn't
quite plan well enough on His own, especially when He had promised to deliver the impossible.

> Now Sarai, Abram's wife had borne him no children,
> and she had an Egyptian maid whose name was Hagar.
> So Sarai said to Abram, "Now behold, the LORD has
> prevented me from bearing children. Please go in to my
> maid; perhaps I will obtain children through her." And

Abram listened to the voice of Sarai. After Abram had lived ten years in the land of Canaan, Abram's wife Sarai took Hagar the Egyptian, her maid, and gave her to her husband Abram as his wife. He went in to Hagar, and she conceived; and when she saw that she had conceived, her mistress was despised in her sight. And Sarai said to Abram, "May the wrong done me be upon you. I gave my maid into your arms, but when she saw that she had conceived, I was despised in her sight. May the LORD judge between you and me" (Genesis 16:1-5).

Sarah knew that God had promised to make Abraham a great nation, yet she also knew that as his wife, she hadn't been able to produce a child for him. So Sarah decided to turn to a human solution in order to bring about a supernatural promise. And because she did that, Sarah changed neighborhoods from *The Real Housewives of Canaan* to *Desperate Housewives*, with all of the drama that came with the new show. A conflict quickly arose between Sarah and her handmaid, Hagar, as well as with Abraham simply because Sarah had involved someone in God's plan that God had never said to include. God had made a promise. He hadn't stuttered. Yet Sarah sought to bring about the product of God's promise in her own way.

Many of us are a lot like Sarah. In fact, God has made promises to us that haven't been realized in our own lives because we tried to take things into our own hands rather than allow God to carry out His own plan.

Did you know that God has given more than 3000 specific promises to His children and recorded them in the Bible? That's enough promises to have a brand-new promise every day for more than a decade. Yet God's promises haven't come to pass in many of our lives because, like Sarah, we keep turning to human solutions to help God out. We look at His promises and make the assumption that God is obviously not living in the real world, because if He were, He would know that what He promised doesn't happen in the real world. In the real world, we're faced with real barrenness, real challenges, real heartache, real health issues, real strongholds, real brokenness, real layoffs, real bills, real betrayals, and real despair. And rather than trust God to come through on His Word, we frequently doubt Him by trying to make things happen on our own.

Just as Sarah did.

Yet so important is this issue of what Sarah did that thousands of years later, the apostle Paul picks up the story to emphasize a point. Paul wants to make unmistakably clear that as followers of Jesus Christ, we are not to force things to happen through human effort but rather to live under the freedom of the promise.

> Tell me, you who want to be under law, do you not listen to the law? For it is written that Abraham had two sons, one by the bondwoman and one by the free woman. But the son by the bondwoman was born according to the flesh, and the son by the free woman through the promise…But what does the Scripture say? "Cast out the bondwoman and her son, for the son of the bondwoman shall not be an heir with the son of the free woman." So then, brethren, we are not children of a bondwoman, but of the free woman (Galatians 4:21-23,30-31).

In other words, Paul urges us as believers not to live our lives in bondage to the ways of our flesh. We are not to try to experience God according to a Hagar mentality. When we try to help God out by using a human approach to solve a divine problem, we lose or delay the divine solution that God has in store for us.

Friend, I have one piece of advice for you—don't go "Hagar" on God. It's easy to do just that when God doesn't appear to be making sense or to be coming through on His promise, but appealing to the flesh will not gain the promises of the Spirit. Rather, appealing to the flesh will create chaos, disorder, and disunity in whatever circumstance, situation, or relationship you're facing.

Just as it did with Sarah.

A number of painful years would pass as Sarah watched Ishmael, the child born to her servant Hagar, grow up before her. Every time Sarah heard Ishmael laugh or every time she saw him run past her tent during his daily activities, she was reminded of the choice she had made. Not only that, but she was also reminded of the promise God had made—to make Abraham into a great nation—and her failure as his wife to provide him with a child of that promise.

Day in and day out, year in and year out, Sarah only grew older. In fact, 25 years would pass between the announcement of God's promise and its fulfillment. After 25 years of pain, emptiness, confusion, and obvious feelings of failure—even though they had tried everything humanly possible to bring God's promise into life—Abraham and Sarah still didn't have a child. And by looking at their response to God's next statement to them about their promised child, it appears that neither of them considered that having a child was even a possibility anymore.

> Now when Abram was ninety-nine years old, the LORD appeared to Abram and said to him, "I am God Almighty; walk before Me, and be blameless. I will establish My covenant between Me and you, and I will multiply you exceedingly…"
>
> Then God said to Abraham, "As for Sarai your wife, you shall not call her name Sarai, but Sarah shall be her name. I will bless her, and indeed I will give you a son by her. Then I will bless her, and she shall be a mother of nations; kings of peoples will come from her." Then Abraham fell on his face and laughed, and said in his heart. "Will a child be born to a man one hundred years old? And will Sarah, who is ninety years old, bear a child?"

And Abraham said to God, "Oh that Ishmael might live before You!" (Gensis 17:1-2,15-18).

God changing Sarai's name to Sarah in this passage is significant. In the Bible, naming something was more than a matter of nomenclature. Naming something created or defined its identity.

The name Sarah literally means "princess" or "noblewoman." God clearly said that kings of peoples would come from Sarah. In order for a king to be a king, he must come from a royal line. In changing Sarai's name to Sarah, God established Sarah as a royal "mother of nations." God specifically declared that something incredibly special was going to happen through Sarah. In doing so, God gave Sarah much more than a name. He gave Sarah her destiny.

But at 90 years of age, Sarah's destiny didn't look like a plausible reality. If Sarah couldn't get pregnant at the age of 65, how did waiting an additional 25 years make it more likely that she could conceive a child by Abraham? To the average viewer of Sarah's drama, her destiny appeared to be no more than a dream.

But God wasn't finished with Sarah. She was empty. She was barren. She had even acted unwisely a decade or so earlier by using the flesh to try to bring about a spiritual promise. But God said that Sarah was His chosen princess through whom He was going to establish His covenant with Abraham.

God had said it, yet judging from Abraham's response to God's revelation, Abraham hadn't believed it. We just read that "Abraham fell on his face and laughed." To make it even worse, Abraham mocked God in his heart by asking, "Will a child be born to a man one hundred years old? And will Sarah, who is ninety years old, bear a child?"

God had just told Abraham that Sarah was going to have a baby, and all Abraham could do was break out into hysterical laughter. "Good one, God," Abraham joked. "I'm ninety-nine, and Sarah is ninety. We couldn't get the shop working twenty-five years ago when

You first told us the news, and You think that all of a sudden we're just going to get this thing rolling? Right, God. I think You meant to say my son Ishmael."

However, God knew exactly what He had meant to say because He corrected Abraham in the very next verse: "No, but Sarah your wife will bear you a son, and you shall call his name Isaac; and I will establish My covenant with him for an everlasting covenant for his descendants after him" (Genesis 17:19).

Later, when God gave more specific details about the promised birth of Abraham's child by Sarah, Sarah overheard the conversation. Her response was no different from her husband's.

> And Sarah was listening at the tent door, which was behind him. Now Abraham and Sarah were old, advanced in age; Sarah was past childbearing. Sarah laughed to herself, saying "After I have become old, shall I have pleasure, my lord being old also?" And the LORD said to Abraham, "Why did Sarah laugh, saying 'Shall I indeed bear a child, when I am so old?' Is anything too difficult for the LORD?" (Genesis 18:10-14).

Abraham laughed. Sarah laughed. Abraham and Sarah seem to be the laughing couple. Neither of them believed God could do what He said He was going to do. In fact, Sarah went so far as to say that she wasn't the only problem—Abraham couldn't even get that far. Super Viagra couldn't help this man out. Sarah said, "After I have become old, shall I have pleasure, my lord being old also?" Sarah laughed at the very thought of becoming pregnant by Abraham.

Notice that Sarah "laughed to herself." I imagine this is similar to what we do as well. We boldly say our "amens" in church and speak with words of faith, but inside we're laughing just like Abraham and Sarah. We're questioning God. But whether we laugh out loud or quietly doesn't matter to God. He hears us clearly either way.

Just as He heard Sarah.

"Why did you laugh?" God asked.

"I didn't laugh," Sarah replied.

"Oh, yes you did," God corrected her. "I heard you."

Sarah had laughed because she didn't think God understood the facts. The facts were that she was old, Abraham was old, and nothing could change that. Those were the facts. But the facts and the promise don't always line up. In fact, rarely do the facts and the promise ever line up. Instead, the facts often challenge our faith that God will fulfill His promise. They are real, right in our face, and relevant. There is no denying the facts. However, the question to ask when you are faced with your own Sarah-like situation is this: Are you going to believe the facts, or are you going to believe the promise?

Don't misunderstand the question. I'm not asking if you are going to believe that the facts are true. The facts *are* true, just as they were true with Sarah. Sarah hadn't had a baby. She was past childbearing age—by a long shot. Abraham no longer gave her any pleasure, if you know what I mean. Women don't get pregnant at the age of 90. Men don't get women pregnant at the age of 100. Those are the facts, and they are true.

But when it comes to God's Word and His promises, the facts alone don't tell the whole story—unless you let them. Don't let yourself get too caught up in the facts. God is trying to get you to embrace the promise.

Much of the time, if not most of the time, God delays the fulfillment of His promise until you're no longer tied to the facts. Just as Israel took 40 years to cover ground that should have taken them 35 days, you can wander in a circle of unbelief until you're ready to trust God.

Often we get frustrated with God because we feel as if He's delaying coming through for us in a situation. Yet when we find ourselves in a situation like that, we need to ask whether God might be delaying because we're too hung up on the facts.

The facts are the facts. I'm not saying that you should dismiss the facts or deny them. Just never let the facts override the promise because *God is greater than the facts.*

Facts alone will lock you into a natural frame of mind, but faith alone will move you into a supernatural one. God's ways are not our ways, but He will let us delay our destiny if we're too focused on doing things our way simply because we can't imagine any other way.

God's Power Revealed

Although Abraham and Sarah laughed when God told them what He would do through them, they had been introduced to a greater level of God's power this second time around. Twenty-five years had passed since God first made His promise known, and two major events had taken place. In these two events, God revealed to Abraham and Sarah just how powerful He is.

The first event took place in Sodom and Gomorrah. When God destroyed the two major powerhouse cities of Sodom and Gomorrah, He showed Abraham and Sarah that nothing is too difficult for Him.

We read about the second event in Genesis 20. Abraham and Sarah traveled "toward the land of the Negev, and settled between Kadesh and Shur" (verse 1). While there, Abraham and Sarah journeyed to Gerar, where the King of Gerar, Abimelech, took a liking to Sarah. Advanced in years, Sarah was still apparently turning heads. Fearing for his own life if the king should find out he was Sarah's husband, Abraham had lied and told him Sarah was his sister. Sarah was Abraham's half-sister, so he told a half-lie—which is pretty much the same as drinking a cup of water that is half-poisoned. It was still a lie.

However, when Abimelech took Sarah into his harem, he went to sleep and had a dream. In his dream, God told him that Sarah was married to Abraham and that he needed to return her to him or he was going to be a dead man. Abimelech immediately returned

Sarah to Abraham, but not before having experienced repercussions from his decision to take her in the first place.

> Abraham prayed to God, and God healed Abimelech and his wife and his maids, so that they bore children. For the LORD had closed fast all the wombs of the household of Abimelech because of Sarah, Abraham's wife (verses 17-18).

Keep Sarah's problem in mind as you think about that passage. Sarah was barren. Her womb had been closed, making it impossible for her to have children. In Gerar, God showed her that He could not only close the womb of every woman in Abimelech's household but also open it back up again. God was demonstrating to Sarah that nothing was impossible for Him.

These two very significant events happened during the 25 years between God's promise that He was going to make Abraham and Sarah into a great nation and the announcement that He was about to fulfill that promise. God showed His power to nurture Abraham and Sarah's faith so it could germinate and grow. He did this because if they didn't believe, He would not bring about the miracle He had promised. As I mentioned when we looked at Rahab's story, faith is God's love language. The writer of Hebrews tells us plainly, "Without faith it is impossible to please Him, for he who comes to God must believe that He is and that He is a rewarder of those who seek Him" (Hebrews 11:6).

Faith is so critical to God that He will intentionally take you through various scenarios and difficulties in order to build your faith. Not only that, He will wait as long as it takes for that faith to bring forth life. God will allow you to remain barren, lifeless, and empty until faith rises from the ashes of doubt. Only then will you experience the abundant life—the spiritual pregnancy that God wants to give you in the midst of your barren and empty situation.

Just as He did for Sarah.

We read in Genesis 21:1, "Then the LORD took note of Sarah as He had said, and the LORD did for Sarah as He had promised." When studying passages in the Bible, I always point out the word *then*. Anytime you see the word *then*, you need to ask yourself, when? Looking back at the previous verses, we discover that God opened up Sarah's womb *after* He had shut and then reopened the wombs in Abimelech's household. God revealed to Sarah His power to control whose wombs are open and whose wombs are closed. *Then* Sarah "conceived and bore a son to Abraham in his old age, at the appointed time of which God had spoken to him" (verse 2).

Sarah had a baby. By Abraham. This undoubtedly produced a spin-off from *The Real Housewives of Canaan* and *Desperate Housewives*. The brand-new show might have been called *Sarah and Abe Plus One*.

I have a feeling that the new show might have been a comedy of sorts because shortly after Sarah had given birth, she named her son Isaac and said, "God has made laughter for me; everyone who hears will laugh with me" (verse 6). This is one laughing family. Sarah said what she did because Isaac's name literally means "he laughs."

God told Abraham he was going to have a son, and Abraham laughed. Sarah overheard God saying she was going to have a son, and Sarah laughed. Isaac's name would now serve as a continual reminder for everyone that nothing is impossible with God—and that God Himself must have a pretty healthy sense of humor too.

Sarah had doubted God's promise. Initially, she had tried using a human solution to solve a heavenly dilemma. Later, she simply lacked the faith to believe that what God had said was actually true. Only after Sarah witnessed God's mighty hand while she was in a foreign land did her faith prompt her to cooperate with the promise. Keep in mind that Sarah didn't get pregnant without responding to a step of faith first.

A Faith That Sees

The principle of faith that applied to Sarah applies to you and me as well. If you are a believer in Jesus Christ, His promises to you are yours by faith. Don't be limited to the facts. Don't be limited to what you can see. We read more about this in Romans 4:16-17:

> For this reason it is by faith, in order that it may be in accordance with grace, so that the promise will be guaranteed to all the descendants, not only to those who are of the Law, but also to those who are of the faith of Abraham, who is the father of us all, (as it is written, "A father of many nations have I made you") in the presence of Him whom he believed, even God, who gives life to the dead and calls into being that which does not exist.

God is so good at being God that He doesn't even need raw materials to work with. God can call into being "that which does not exist." He can take dead things and give them life. He can miraculously intervene and cause a dead womb to house new life. He can give a dead future new life. Or a dead career, a dead dream, or a dead heart. God is a master at bringing life from what appears to have died. When God brings into being that which does not exist, we call that *ex nihilo*. That simply means that God creates something out of nothing.

If you have a dead hope, a dead relationship, or even a dead dream, God has a way of making life come out of something that doesn't even exist. Don't look at what you can see. Don't just look at the facts.

Maybe you have been single for a long time, and you have given up believing that your future spouse is out there somewhere. Remember that God doesn't need raw materials to work with. You don't need to invent a way to meet a man or meet a woman, such as going to a club or hanging out somewhere that might not be the best place for you. God is so good at what He does, if you will simply trust Him in faith and stop looking to human solutions to solve a spiritual issue, God can bring your future spouse directly to you. He can create families, careers, futures, and good health even when He didn't seem to have anything at all to work with. Trust Him.

In fact, do more than trust Him. Do what Abraham did. In Romans 4:18, we read, "In hope against hope he believed, so that he might become a father of many nations."

Doesn't that sound like a conundrum of sorts? Abraham hoped against hope. It was a hope set against all odds. That means he hoped when there was no hope to be had. Abraham believed when there was no belief to be found. I don't want you to read that too quickly and miss the significance of this verse. In a *hopeless* situation, Abraham *hoped.* Paul wants us to clearly understand that Abraham faced more than just a difficult situation with Sarah. Paul wants us to know beyond the shadow of a doubt that Abraham hoped *against all hope.*

And because of that hope, Abraham took a step of faith.

> Without becoming weak in faith he contemplated his own body, now as good as dead since he was about a hundred years old, and the deadness of Sarah's womb; yet, with respect to the promise of God, he did not waver in unbelief but grew strong in faith, giving glory to God, and being fully assured that what God had promised, He was able also to perform (Romans 4:19-21).

To contemplate is to think about something. Without getting into too many personal details, Abraham is laying in his bed at night contemplating the fact that his own body is "as good as dead." Yet he remembers God's promise that Sarah is going to bear his son. On one hand, Abraham doesn't want to be physically intimate with his wife because he thinks, "What's the use? My body is dead. Sarah's womb is closed. Go to sleep, Abe. Goodnight."

But on the other hand, Abraham remembers what God has said. He remembers the power God displayed at Sodom and Gomorrah as well as in his experience with King Abimelech. Those thoughts then make Abraham want to try to be physically intimate.

Abraham thought about his problem.

Then Abraham thought about God's promise.

He thought again about his problem.

Then he thought again about God's promise.

And Scripture says that when Abraham gave glory to God in the middle of his problem, he decided to be intimate with his wife. Nine months later, baby Isaac was born.

Abraham's response should be our own. Never let the problem dictate what you are going to do. Instead, act with a full view of the promise. And nine months later—or however short or long—you can testify to what God has done in and through you.

Against All Hope

Even though Abraham and Sarah lost a number of years when Sarah came up with a human plan to force God's promise, God ultimately delivered on what He had told them with a special delivery of His own. God might have seemed to be taking a long time, but He was waiting until all of the pieces were in place—waiting until Abraham was able to hope against all hope and Sarah was able to respond in faith—in order to bring about the fruition of His promise.

If God seems to be taking too long to come through for you, I want to encourage you to keep believing. Don't give up. Don't throw in the towel. God isn't working on your timetable, and He is not bound by your facts. Trust Him.

"But Tony," I can hear you saying, "I'm so old now—even if God does come through, my life is pretty much over at this point, or my family is grown, or I'm forty years old and I'm not married yet…if God comes through now, it's too late anyhow."

Friend, it's never too late. Take courage because Sarah might have had the same thought. After all, she was 90 years old when she had Isaac. Could she expect to see him become a toddler, a teenager, or a young adult? Most of us would assume that she could not. But Genesis 23:1 says that "Sarah lived one hundred and twenty-seven years; these were the years of the life of Sarah." Sarah is the only woman in the Bible whose age is given at her death. That is something frequently done for men, but no other woman in the Bible has her age of death recorded.

One reason God may have wanted us to know this is to remind us that even though He might seem to be taking a long time to come through with His promise, when He does come through, He's going to give you enough time to enjoy it. Sarah got to live 37 more years after Isaac was born. That's a lot of birthday parties and Mother's Day cards.

The latter part of Sarah's life reminds me of another biblical character who could have been discouraged that the best years of his life were wasted in wandering—through no fault of his own.

Caleb and Joshua were two of the twelve spies we mentioned in the introduction. These two said that the Israelites should enter the Promised Land as God had told them. However, the remainder of the Israelites voted them down, forcing them to suffer the punishment of those who had lacked faith. For 40 years, Caleb and Joshua wandered in the desert because other people's unbelief had prevented them from going where God had told them they could go.

However, instead of bemoaning the years he lost and settling in a rocking chair by a fire pit once the Israelites eventually got to enter the Promised Land, Caleb said to Joshua, "Give me that mountain!" He actually had a bit more to say than just that.

> "I was forty years old when Moses the servant of the
> LORD sent me from Kadesh-barnea to spy out the land,
> and I brought word back to him as it was in my heart.

Nevertheless my brethren who went up with me made the heart of the people melt with fear; but I followed the LORD my God fully. So Moses swore on that day, saying, 'Surely the land on which your foot has trodden will be an inheritance to you and to your children forever, because you have followed the LORD my God fully.' Now behold, the LORD has let me live, just as He spoke, these forty-five years, from the time that the LORD spoke this word to Moses, when Israel walked in the wilderness; and now behold, I am eighty-five years old today. *I am still as strong today as I was in the day Moses sent me; as my strength was then, so my strength is now, for war and for going out and coming in.* Now then, give me this hill country about which the LORD spoke on that day, for you heard on that day that Anakim were there, with great fortified cities; perhaps the LORD will be with me, and I will drive them out as the LORD has spoken."

So Joshua blessed him and gave Hebron to Caleb the son of Jephunneh for an inheritance (Joshua 14:7-13).

Caleb didn't allow his past to determine his future. Caleb had lost a lot of years in the wilderness though he had done nothing wrong. Maybe something similar has happened to you. Maybe you feel as if decades have gone by, and you haven't been able to get to the place you believed God told you He was taking you. It could be because of a sin someone committed against you, or a duty you felt obligated to fulfill, or any number of things. However, if anyone had a reason to complain, 85-year-old Caleb did. Yet not even a hint of looking back appears in his words. Rather, Caleb—no doubt slightly bent over by then from age—is ready to take on the titanically oversized Anakim without hesitation or concern.

History goes on to show that Caleb was able to drive the Anakim out of his land. Recorded in Joshua and Judges, Caleb's victory is clear.

> Caleb drove out from there the three sons of Anak: Shes-
> hai and Ahiman and Talmai, the children of Anak (Joshua
> 15:14).

> Then they gave Hebron to Caleb, as Moses had prom-
> ised; and he drove out from there the three sons of Anak
> (Judges 1:20).

Caleb didn't let lost years keep him from gaining what had been promised or from *enjoying* it. He is like Sarah, who got to enjoy the fulfillment of her promise for many years as well. In fact, Sarah's comeback was so strong that she ended up in the Hall of Faith. "By faith even Sarah herself received ability to conceive, even beyond the proper time of life, since she considered Him faithful who had promised" (Hebrews 11:11).

Sarah will forever be remembered as a role model for all women.

> For in this way in former times the holy women also, who
> hoped in God, used to adorn themselves, being submis-
> sive to their own husbands; just as Sarah obeyed Abra-
> ham, calling him lord, and you have become her children
> if you do what is right without being frightened by any
> fear (1 Peter 3:5-6).

God used Sarah's faith and obedience to turn what seemed like a hopeless situation and a devastating mistake into a legacy to be cher-ished. If God did it with Sarah, He can do it with you.

Regardless of the reason why you may not have experienced the fulfillment of God's promise to you—even if someone else's unbe-lief or sin interfered with your life—your past doesn't have to dictate what God has for you now and the time He will give you to enjoy His blessing in the future.

It's okay to recognize the facts of your situation. And those facts might not look all that good. But don't miss the promise you have of a future and a hope.

Don't miss that.

Never limit God through unbelief. Give Him the opportunity to amaze you. Let Him surprise you. Let God make you say, "Wow! Who knew He had it in Him to pull that off for me!"

God *does* have it in Him. I know He does. I've seen Him do it in the lives of the people we've studied throughout these pages. You have seen it too. But more than that, I have seen Him do it in my own life as well. And I am still believing that He will do more. At the time of this writing, I am 63 years old—just as strong now as I have ever been. I want that mountain God has told me about.

I want you to have your mountain too.

Trust Him for it. Trust Him to guide you on the path He has for your life. If you will trust Him, responding in faith and obedience to His Word, He won't let you down. Those who hope in God will never be disappointed (Isaiah 49:23).

I promise.

Better yet, *He* promises. It's never too late to take Him at His Word.

A Final Word:
Rebounding in Life

Over the past 30 years, one of the highlights of my ministry has been serving as the chaplain for the NBA Dallas Mavericks. If you've ever been to a professional basketball game, you know that each minute is filled with energy, sweat, determination, and the finest of athletic skill. Teams battle for the prize of being declared that night's victor. Players run, fake, shoot, and block in an effort to get a ball through a rim as many times as possible.

One element of the game that makes basketball so intriguing is the rebound. A rebound occurs anytime there is a missed shot or a missed free throw. In the case of an offensive rebound, anyone on the offense grabs the ball after it bounces off the rim and puts it up again or runs another play. Rather than giving up possession of the ball, a rebound retains possession, giving the offense another chance to score.

If the game of basketball didn't have the option of the rebound, it would slow down considerably. The pressure underneath the basket would greatly diminish. And missed shots would be all the more painful to swallow. Rebounds allow the players to take a bad situation and make it good again.

What a rebound does in the game of basketball, God does in the game of life by giving another chance after a failed attempt. A rebound is a do-over. It proves that even in life, it's not too late to try again.

Over the previous eight chapters, you and I have experienced the ups and downs of those who made a rebound. We've seen a murderer become a deliverer. We've seen a harlot end up in the messianic line. We've seen a trickster turn into a patriarch, a rebel into an evangelist, and a diva into a deliverer. We've seen a traitor triumph over his fears, a player deal the last hand, and a doubter ushered into the Hall of Faith through her belief in God's promise of a son.

Each of these individuals could have given up when things looked bad. Each could have walked away. Each could have thrown in the towel, sat down on the bench, or just plain quit. But none did. Instead, each took a difficult situation and tried again—this time with faith. And as a result of their faith, they all ended up scoring with nothing but net.

In the Christian life, just as in basketball, a missed shot does not mean the game is over. If there is still time left on the clock (and we know there is because you are still here), it's not too late for a rebound.

But you need to keep in mind what every good basketball player knows as well—in order to get a rebound, you need to position yourself in the vicinity of the basket. You can't be on the other side of the court, in the stands, or in the parking lot and expect to grab the rebound. Neither can you, as a believer in Jesus Christ, be removed from a close and abiding relationship with Him and expect to experience His divine restoration to your situation.

As famed NBA rebounder Larry Byrd has said, "Most rebounds are taken below the rim. That's where I get mine." Knowing this, Byrd intentionally positions himself near the rim because the key to a successful rebound is to be where you can move forward once you grab the ball. Likewise, the key to a successful rebound in the

Christian life is to position yourself underneath the comprehensive rule of God. When you align yourself with God's rule—what I refer to as God's kingdom agenda—you are in the best position for your rebound.

Maybe you're thinking this principle will work for others but not for you. "If I were Larry Byrd, I could rebound too." It's true that Larry Byrd may have an advantage over most of us when rebounding a basketball. And some people may have an advantage over you in rebounding from life's situations because they may not have experienced the depth of your pain, shame, or disappointments.

I'm not going to diminish what you've gone through, what you have done, or what you may be up against. Neither am I going to deny that getting a rebound is a lot easier for someone like Larry Byrd than it is for someone like you or me. But let me direct your attention to someone else. He is someone I have had the thrill of watching on the Mavericks team over the past several years, someone whose hope and tenacity should be a model for our own.

His name is Jason Kidd. If you don't follow basketball closely, you may not have heard of him. If you were to run into the Mavericks team at a restaurant or an event, you may even miss seeing him altogether. After all, most of the players tower over Kidd causing him to appear somewhat like his name—a kid. At his height and weight, Kidd can disappear next to the Mavericks' giants, like Dirk Nowitzki, who stand at seven feet.

But don't let Kidd's size fool you. In his rookie year in 1994, he rallied the Mavericks from the worst record in the league the year before to the best improvement in the NBA for that year. And even though he played on a team with a losing record, Kidd still managed to tie for the NBA Rookie of the Year with Grant Hill of the Pistons.

A decade later, and having been traded to the New York Nets, Kidd was credited with having resurrected the nearly dead Nets with one of the greatest turnarounds in NBA history. His first year with the Nets, Kidd led them to their first-ever showing in the NBA finals.

Fast-forward a few more years, and Kidd has come back home to the Mavericks. A consistent player in all arenas, Kidd didn't let what many would consider a disadvantage—his lack of height—stop him from not only grabbing multiple rebounds but also scoring with them. In fact, Kidd has more than 7,000 rebounds. He's the *only* player in NBA history with the combined record of more than 15,000 points, 10,000 assists, and 7,000 rebounds. Did you catch that? The short Kidd holds a very tall record. Translation: You don't have to be a Byrd to fly. You just have to believe, position yourself, and never cease to try.

God has a million ways to hit a bull's eye with a crooked stick, or like Kidd recently did, make a 75-foot shot with only seconds left in the game—on a rebound.

Friend, if you hear nothing else from our time together in these pages, hear this: *It's not too late.* Don't let your circumstances, where you have been, what you have done, who has done what to you, or what you are up against dictate the final outcome of your game. Rather, let the One who can make all things brand-new position you underneath the covering of His overarching rule.

You *will* rebound there. You *will* score. You *will* live the life that God has in store. Not because of you and the great things you have done, but because of the faith you have placed in His Son.

Have you missed a shot—or two, or three, or ten? Last time I checked, the game is still on. Grab your rebound. It's not too late for you to win.

Questions for Discussion or Personal Reflection

Introduction

1. Name one experience or personal decision from your past that has shaped you in positive ways. Now name one piece of baggage from your past that you would like to leave behind.

2. Finish this sentence: It's not too late for me to...

Chapter 1: Moses Was a Murderer

1. Have you ever had a dream for your life? What is the status of that dream—fulfilled? In process? Gone?

2. Have you ever tried to fulfill a dream, only to have the experience go terribly wrong?

3. Have you ever had a "wilderness" experience—an extended time-out, or a time when you felt as if you were on the sidelines of life? If so, can you identify one positive effect that time had on you?

4. Name one long-standing situation or circumstance in your life that you would like to see changed.

5. You've probably never seen a bush that was on fire but not consumed, but have you seen God "show up" in your life in some other way? How?

Chapter 2: Rahab Was a Harlot

1. Rahab was labeled a harlot. What label have you worn? What might God think about that label?

2. Rahab took a risk by hiding the spies. Have you ever taken a risky step of faith? Are you considering one now? Explain.

3. If God's love language is faith, name one practical way you can express your love for God today.

4. Rahab had to go against her culture in order to follow God. Have you had to do that? How?

5. Have any "walls" collapsed around you? In what way are you trusting God to deliver you?

Chapter 3: Jacob Was a Liar

1. Have you ever had to wait a *long* time for something you really wanted? How did you change during the waiting period?

2. What does it mean to wrestle with God today? Have you ever felt as if you were wrestling with God? What was the situation?

3. God dislocated Jacob's hip with one touch. What painful experience has God used to shape your character? What effect has that experience had on you?

4. God gave Jacob a new name—Israel. Have you ever had a nickname? Have you ever felt as if others labeled you? What label would you like to wear?

5. Jacob's wrestling match with God was a defining moment in his life. Have you had any defining moments with God? Explain.

6. Think of one way God has blessed you. How can you pass that blessing along to others?

Chapter 4: Jonah Was a Rebel

1. Have you ever felt as if God was asking you to do something you didn't want to do? What happened?

2. Have you ever tried running from God or from His will for you? How did that work out?

3. In the belly of the fish, Jonah finally repented. Have your decisions ever led you to a dark and lonely place? What was your response?

4. Do you know people who seem extremely unlikely to respond to God? How might God be working behind the scenes to reveal Himself to them?

5. Have you ever been angry with God?

6. In what way have you received God's grace? In what way might He be asking you to be a dispenser of grace?

Chapter 5: Esther Was a Diva

1. How has God manifested His providence in your life? Can you think of an apparent coincidence or a mistake that God used to accomplish His will in your life—a time when God was working behind the scenes in your situation?

2. Not everyone is chosen to be queen, but everyone does have influence on others. Who might you be influencing? What might God intend to accomplish through you?

3. People can act like divas even if they aren't kings or queens. What divalike attitudes or actions do we need to guard against in our everyday lives? In other

words, in what ways might you be tempted to play the diva card?

4. How might God's blessings in your life be making you more useful in the kingdom? In other words, how can you connect your blessings to God's purpose?

5. Esther risked her life to share her blessings with her people. Have you ever taken a risk to share your blessings with others? What risk might you need to take in the future?

6. Because of Haman, Esther was in a seemingly hopeless situation. Have you ever seen God turn around a situation that appeared hopeless? What happened?

Chapter 6: Peter Was an Apostate

1. Dr. Evans writes, "We can dignify our difficulties by discovering the destiny God is taking us to through the trial." What do you think it means to "dignify our difficulties"? Are you experiencing any difficulties that you can "dignify"?

2. Dr. Evans writes, "Satan often looks to bring us down in the very area where we would never imagine we could fall." How can we be strong in the Lord without being arrogant or overconfident?

3. Have you ever felt as if you let down the Lord? Afterward, did you feel like running away from Jesus or running to Him? Do our failures change the way God feels about us?

4. Imagine Jesus asking you, "Do you love Me with a committed, self-sacrificing love?" How would you respond to Him?

5. After Peter's failure and restoration, he was better prepared to fulfill his ministry. If you have experienced failure and restoration, can you identify any positive changes that have occurred in your life as a result?

Chapter 7: Samson Was a Player

1. As a Nazirite, Samson was set apart. In what ways are believers set apart (or sanctified) today?

2. Samson's life was characterized by compromise. Have you had to face the temptation to compromise? Explain.

3. "When we try to mix worldly standards with God's values, we end up alienating ourselves from the one true God and losing His presence and His power in our lives, just as Samson did." What worldly standards have you had to reject in order to enjoy God's presence and power? What worldly standards might you have to reject in the future?

4. Samson was empowered when he acted according to his calling. Have you ever sensed God's power flowing through you to accomplish something you couldn't accomplish on your own? Explain.

5. Samson's greatest victory came at the end of his life. Is there something that you are looking forward to God accomplishing through you?

Chapter 8: Sarah Was a Doubter

1. How would you describe the difference between a barren life and an abundant life? Have you experienced times of each? Explain.

2. Have you ever tried to help God out—to fulfill His promises on your own rather than waiting on Him? If so, what happened?

3. Sarah felt like a failure even though her barrenness wasn't her fault. Think of a time when you've felt like a failure. As you recall that situation, what might God be communicating to you through Sarah's example?

4. Abraham and Sarah both laughed at God's promise. Have you ever struggled to take a promise from God seriously? What was the situation?

5. Abraham had hope in the midst of a hopeless situation. If you are facing a seemingly hopeless situation, how might you express your hope?

6. After her test of faith, Sarah made a strong comeback, becoming a role model and leaving a legacy of faith. What legacy would you like to leave behind someday?

Scripture Index

About Dr. Tony Evans

Dr. Tony Evans is the founder and president of the Urban Alternative, a ministry dedicated to restoring hope through teaching God's Word. He is also the founder and senior pastor of the 9000-member Oak Cliff Bible Fellowship in Dallas. His radio broadcast, *The Alternative with Dr. Tony Evans,* can be heard on more than 1000 US outlets daily and in more than 130 countries. He is a dynamic speaker and author and serves as chaplain to the NBA Dallas Mavericks.

If you've enjoyed *It's Not Too Late,* be sure to
read Dr. Evans' powerful book on spiritual warfare...

Victory in Spiritual Warfare
Outfitting Yourself for the Battle

In this timely, unique exploration of spiritual warfare, Dr. Evans unveils a simple yet radical truth: Every struggle and conflict faced in the physical realm has its root in the spiritual realm.

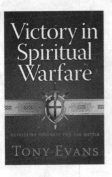

With passion and clarity, Dr. Evans demystifies spiritual warfare so that you can tackle challenges and obstacles with spiritual power—God's authority—as you...

- understand how the battle is fought by Satan
- actively use the armor of God
- find strength in prayer and sufficiency in Christ
- win over chemical, sexual, emotional, relational, and other strongholds

The Urban Alternative

Dr. Tony Evans and the Urban Alternative (TUA) equips, empowers, and unites Christians to impact individuals, families, churches, and communities to restore hope and transform lives.

We believe the core cause of the problems we face in our personal lives, homes, and societies is a spiritual one; therefore, the only way to address them is spiritually. We've tried political, social, economic, and even religious agendas. It's time for a Kingdom Agenda—God's visible and comprehensive rule over every area of life—because when we function as we were designed, God's divine power changes everything. It renews and restores as the life of Christ is made manifest within our own. As we align ourselves under Him, there is an alignment that happens from deep within, and He brings about full restoration. It is an atmosphere that revives and makes whole.

As it impacts us, it impacts others, transforming every sphere of life. When each biblical sphere of life functions in accordance with God's Word, the outcomes are evangelism, discipleship, and community impact. As we learn how to govern ourselves under God, we transform the institutions of family, church, and society according to a biblically based kingdom perspective. Through Him, we touch heaven and change earth.

To achieve our goal we use a variety of strategies, methods, and resources for reaching and equipping as many people as possible.

Broadcast Media

Hundreds of thousands of individuals experience *The Alternative with Dr. Tony Evans* through the daily radio broadcast playing on more than 1000 US outlets and in more than 130 countries. The broadcast can also be seen on several television networks and at TonyEvans.org.

Leadership Training

The Kingdom Agenda Pastors (KAP) provides a viable network for like-minded pastors who embrace the Kingdom Agenda philosophy. Pastors have the opportunity to go deeper with Dr. Tony Evans as they are given greater biblical knowledge, practical applications, and resources to impact individuals, families, churches, and communities. KAP welcomes senior and associate pastors of all churches.

The Kingdom Agenda Pastors Biannual Summit progressively develops church leaders to meet the demands of the twenty-first century while maintaining the Gospel message and the strategic position of the church. The Summit introduces intensive seminars, workshops, and resources, addressing issues affecting the community, family, leadership, organizational health, and more.

Pastors' Wives Ministry, founded by Dr. Lois Evans, provides counsel, encouragement, and spiritual resources for pastors' wives as they serve with their husbands in the ministry. A primary focus of the ministry is the biannual KAP Summit, which offers senior pastors' wives a safe place to reflect, renew, and relax along with training in personal development, spiritual growth, and care for their emotional and physical well-being.

Community Impact

National Church Adopt-A-School Initiative (NCAASI) prepares churches across the country to impact communities by using public schools as the primary vehicle for effecting positive social change in urban youth and families. Leaders of churches, school districts, faith-based organizations, and other nonprofit organizations are equipped with the knowledge and tools to forge partnerships and build strong social service delivery systems. This training is based on the comprehensive church-based community impact strategy conducted by Oak Cliff Bible Fellowship. It addresses such areas as economic development, education, housing, health revitalization, family renewal, and racial reconciliation. We also assist churches in tailoring the model to meet the specific needs of their communities while simultaneously addressing the spiritual and moral frame of reference.

Resource Development

We are fostering lifelong learning partnerships with the people we serve by providing a variety of published materials. We offer booklets, Bible studies, books, CDs, and DVDs to strengthen people in their walk with God and ministry to others.

For more information, a catalog
of Dr. Tony Evans' ministry resources,
and a complimentary copy of
Dr. Evans' devotional newsletter,
call

(800) 800-3222

or write

TUA at PO Box 4000, Dallas TX 75208

or log on to

www.TonyEvans.org

To learn more about books by Dr. Tony Evans
or to read sample chapters, visit our website:

www.harvesthousepublishers.com

HARVEST HOUSE PUBLISHERS
EUGENE, OREGON